2

Workboo

Grammar

Connection

STRUCTURE

THROUGH

CONTENT

SERIES EDITORS

Marianne Celce-Murcia

M. E. Sokolik

Hilary Grant

THOMSON
HEINLE

Australia • Canada • Mexico • Singapore • United Kingdom • United States

Grammar Connection 2: Structure Through Content
Workbook
Series Editors: Marianne Celce-Murcia, M. E. Sokolik,
Hilary Grant

Editorial Director: *Joe Dougherty*
Publisher: *Sherrise Roehr*
Consulting Editor: *James W. Brown*
VP, Director of Content Development:
  Anita Raducanu
Acquisitions Editor, Adult & Academic ESL:
  Tom Jefferies
Senior Development Editor: *Michael Ryall*
Editorial Assistant: *Katherine Reilly*
Director of Product Marketing: *Amy Mabley*
Executive Marketing Manager: *Jim McDonough*
Senior Field Marketing Manager:
  Donna Lee Kennedy

Cover Image: ©Robert Harding World Imagery/Getty

Product Marketing Manager: *Katie Kelley*
Senior Content Project Manager:
  Maryellen Eschmann-Killeen
Print Buyer: *Betsy Donaghey*
Production Project Manager: *Chrystie Hopkins*
Production Services: *Parkwood Composition Services*
Cover Designer: *Linda Beaupre*
Printer: *Transcontinental Printing*

For permission to use material from this text or product,
submit a request online at http://www.thomsonrights.com

Any additional questions about permissions can be
submitted by email to thomsonrights@thomson.com

ISBN 13: 978-1-4130-0839-5

Printed in Canada
1 2 3 4 5 6 7 8 9 10 — 11 10 09 08 07

For more information contact Heinle, 25 Thomson
Place, Boston, Massachusetts 02210 USA, or you can
visit our Internet site at http://elt.heinle.com

Contents

The Present and Past of *Be*; *Be* + Nouns or Adjectives

PART ONE	The Present and Past of *Be*

A Complete the statements with the present or the past of *be.* Use contractions when possible.

1. It _____was_____ humid yesterday.

2. They _____ in class now.

3. I (negative) _____ at home last night.

4. Who _____ in the cafeteria in the morning?

5. The weather _____ beautiful on Sunday.

6. _____ it windy outside right now?

7. They (negative) _____ from Canada. They're from the United States.

8. My neighbors _____ on vacation last week.

9. Mary and Scott (negative) _____ students. They're instructors.

10. Juanita _____ my new roommate.

11. We _____ late for class! Hurry up!

12. His birthday _____ two days ago.

B Write questions for the answers.

1. ___*Was the weather windy?*___ Yes, the weather was windy.

2. _____

   Yes, it's cold outside.

3. _____

   No, she isn't our English instructor.

4. _____

   Yes, we were at the movies Monday night.

5. _____

   No, they weren't at the party two weeks ago.

C Answer the yes/no questions.

1. Are you cold now?

   Yes, I am. OR No, I'm not.

2. Was it sunny last week?

   _____

3. Is it usually cool in Cuba?

   _____

4. Were they late for the meeting?

   _____

5. Was it warm and dry in Mumbai last June?

   _____

6. Was your English instructor on vacation last week?

   _____

7. Were you in the United States two years ago?

   _____

PART TWO   *Be* + Nouns or Adjectives

A Unscramble the sentences.

1. in Madrid / warm / it / was

   It was warm in Madrid.

2. nice / my / are / classmates

   _____

3. hurricane / was / deadly / a / Katrina

   _____

4. the / in / Bogotá / is / cool / weather / usually

   _____

5. winds / strong / dangerous / are

   _____

6. were / we / last night / scared

   _____

7. worried / are / my parents / always

   _____

B Complete the sentences to make true statements. Use the verb *be* and an appropriate adjective.

1. My instructor

   _____ My instructor is helpful. _____

2. My neighborhood

   _____

3. The class

   _____

4. My friends

   _____

5. English

   _____

6. The weather in my country

   _____

7. I

   _____

8. Movie stars

   _____

Putting It Together

GRAMMAR

A Rewrite the sentences with mistakes. If there are no mistakes, write "C."

1. It's sunny yesterday.   _____ It was sunny yesterday. _____

2. They're instructors English.   _____

3. They were at the mall last Saturday. _____

4. I from Chile.   _____

5. The northwestern states is rainy.   _____

6. We're at home last night.   _____

7. Was it cold in Florida?   _____

8. How's the weather in your city yesterday? _____

B Complete the conversation with the present and past of *be.* Use the negative where necessary.

Sam: ___Are___ your parents on vacation now?

Jane: Yes. They _____ in Melbourne, Australia.

Sam: _____ it really hot there?

Jane: No, right now it _____ cold in Melbourne.

Sam: Cold in July? _____ it usually hot in Australia?

Jane: No. There are different seasons, but in the north the climate _____ tropical. I love Australia. Last year we _____ in Sydney.

Sam: _____ it cold?

Jane: No, it _____ . We _____ there in January.

C Write about your last vacation.

1. Where were you?

   _____

2. Who was with you?

   _____

3. How was the weather?

   _____

4. What was your hotel like?

   _____

5. How was the food?

   _____

6. Was it a fun vacation?

   _____

Find the words in the puzzle below and circle them.

```
M  X  R  I  Y  C  D  T  M  S  S  J  C  B  W
H  M  R  A  W  L  C  A  I  Y  U  Q  S  I  M
J  M  Q  K  O  N  L  R  Y  D  K  N  N  O  E
D  X  B  C  Z  X  K  M  G  U  A  D  N  P  R
S  Q  A  R  B  X  L  C  U  O  Y  T  Z  Y  N
Z  F  R  K  Y  Q  L  R  M  L  V  A  N  D  H
L  D  T  N  M  G  O  X  B  C  T  X  T  O  Q
N  O  I  J  L  N  O  K  D  R  Y  R  M  R  H
H  A  F  F  V  S  C  H  K  T  H  V  T  Q  T
R  D  Z  Y  B  N  S  C  O  H  U  M  I  D  M
K  E  H  F  I  O  J  G  E  T  G  F  D  M  O
D  W  M  L  T  W  G  W  H  X  K  X  R  H  R
V  L  Z  O  R  Y  U  J  Q  T  X  L  L  N  F
W  L  I  Y  A  N  Q  H  M  Q  T  R  N  M  T
M  T  X  M  M  P  W  N  Q  D  I  Z  Z  F  A
```

CLOUDY

COLD

COOL

DRY

HOT

HUMID

RAINY

SNOWY

SUNNY

WARM

WINDY

L e s s o n ②

Be **in the Past:**
Information Questions;
***What* or *Which* in *Be* Questions**

PART ONE	*Be* **in the Past: Information Questions**

A **Complete the questions with the appropriate question word(s) from the box.**

who	how long	when	how old	how heavy
how far	what	where	why	

1. _____*who*_____ was Albert Einstein?   He was a brilliant scientist.

2. _____ were you last night?   I was at a party.

3. _____ was your favorite subject in
high school?   French.

4. _____ were they late for the meeting?   They were in traffic.

5. _____ was your suitcase?   It was 30 pounds.

6. _____ are you?   I'm 23.

7. _____ was your trip?   14 days.

8. _____ was the airport from your hotel?   Two miles.

9. _____ was your last doctor's appointment?   Two years ago.

B **Circle the correct information word to complete each question.**

1. Where / (What) is London?   A city.

2. Who / What was Magellan?   He was a Portuguese explorer.

3. When / Where was Henry VIII from?   He was from England.

4. How long / How far was the restaurant?   About five miles.

5. Where / How old was the Ottoman Empire?   In Africa, Europe, and the
Middle East.

6. Why / Who was Magellan famous?   He was an early world explorer.

7. What / When were the explorers in the
Philippines?   In 1521.

C Create an information question in the past for each answer.

Raul: _____ *Where were you last night?* _____

Carolina: I was at my birthday party.

Raul: _____

Carolina: My birthday was last week.

Raul: _____

Carolina: My parents were at my birthday party.

Raul: _____

Carolina: My favorite gift was a painting.

Raul: _____

Carolina: Because it's very beautiful and because it's from my country.

PART TWO	*What* or *Which* in *Be* Questions

A Circle *what* or *which* to complete the questions.

1. Amy: I was in three different countries for vacation last year.

   Pablo: What /(Which) country was your favorite?

2. Alana: Look at all my books!

   Rick: What / which book was your favorite?

3. Peter: I have two English instructors. One is from Singapore.

   Ana: What / Which instructor is from Singapore?

4. Isabela: We are on ancient civilizations in history class.

   Solin: What / Which civilization is more interesting to you?

5. Fedor: I was a big music fan when I was a teenager.

   Gerardo: What / which music was your favorite?

6. Angie: A lot of my friends were at the international dinner.

   Berndt: What / Which ones were your friends?

B Write *what* or *which* to complete the questions.

1. _____*what*_____ nationality are your parents?

2. _____ country was your grandfather from?

3. _____ school is your daughter in?

4. _____ college is your son at: Princeton or Yale?

5. _____ student in your class is from Russia?

6. _____ friend of yours is from England: Ian or Nigel?

7. _____ country is Celine Dion from?

8. _____ movies were the best from last year?

9. _____ Greek god is the god of war?

10. _____ pencil is for standardized test taking?

Putting It Together

GRAMMAR

A **Rewrite the sentences with mistakes. If there are no mistakes, write "C."**

1. What was your first teacher?   _Who was your first teacher?_

2. What is your favorite color?   _____

3. What is your favorite car:
   Honda or Chevrolet?   _____

4. Where is the city of Anchorage?   _____

5. When was Bill Clinton president?   _____

6. What was President Clinton like?   _____

7. Which is George W. Bush?   _____

8. Why you here?   _____

9. How far is your great grandfather?   _____

10. Why's he here?   _____

11. Which is better: a Mac or a PC?   _____

B **Complete the conversation with the word(s) from the box. Some words may be used more than once.**

which	were	how old	what	was
when	who	is	are	

Student: _____*who*_____ were the ancient Maya?

Teacher: They _____ a civilization in Central America.

Student: _____ countries in Central America were they from?

Teacher: They _____ from Mexico, Guatemala, Belize, and even Honduras.

Student: _____ is Mayan civilization?

Teacher: Very old. But the most famous period _____ the Classic period.

Student: _____ was the Classic period?

Teacher: It _____ from 250 AD to 900 AD.

Student: _____ was the Classic period?

Teacher: The Classic period was when the Maya had urban centers with pyramids and other structures, but modern Maya _____ still in Central America.

Student: Really?

Teacher: Yes. There are Mayan people in Mexico, Belize, and Guatemala.

C **Answer the questions with information about yourself.**

1. When were you last in your home country?

   _____

2. What was your address in your home country?

   _____

3. Who was your favorite teacher in high school?

   _____

4. Where was your best friend yesterday?

   _____

5. Were you hot in class today?

   _____

6. Was your English instructor on vacation last week?

   _____

7. Were you in the United States two years ago?

   _____

Complete the sentences. Then solve the puzzle.

Across

3. Magellan's _____ took him around the world.

6. Where is the king? On his _____.

7. The Trinidad was a _____.

9. Catholicism is a _____.

Down

1. Elizabeth was an English _____.

2. Magellan was a _____.

4. She paints. She's an _____.

5. A hundred years is a _____.

8. Henry VIII was a _____.

A **Circle the correct preposition to complete the e-mail.**

To: matt@mail.net
Subject: In Bogotá!

Hi Matt:
We're ①in / around Bogotá now. It's an amazing city (2) in / at the Andes
mountains. Bogotá is located 10,000 feet (3) above / below the sea. It's really high!
We're staying (4) at / on a hotel in the north of the city. The hotel is (5) under /
between two major avenues—7th and 11th. There are a lot of shops (6) near /
on the hotel. There are also some shops (7) in / above the hotel. As a matter of
fact, there are shops all (8) around / below us! We aren't (9) far from / between
the center of the city—about a 30-minute car ride. We were there all day today.
Yesterday we were (10) at / in the countryside. We were (11) in / on a farm in a
valley. It was very beautiful.
See you soon!
Hilary

B **Complete the sentences with a preposition from the box.**

near	around	next to	between
on	in	above	far from

1. The fish swim _____*in*_____ the river.

2. The island is _____ two volcanic islands.

3. My house is _____ the train station. It's five minutes away.

4. My friend, Ana, always sits _____ me in class.

5. There are a lot of shells _____ the beach.

6. The airport is _____ my house. It's two hours away.

7. The kite flies high _____ the trees.

8. We were in a boat on a river yesterday. There were alligators all _____ us!

C Describe your classroom using the prepositions of location in parentheses. Write complete sentences.

1. (behind) _____ There is a map behind the teacher's desk. _____

2. (near) _____

3. (between) _____

4. (on) _____

5. (in) _____

6. (far from) _____

7. (around) _____

8. (next to) _____

PART TWO	*There + Be*

A Complete the sentences with *there is/are.*

1. _____ There is _____ a waterfall in the forest.

2. _____ volcanoes in Nicaragua.

3. _____ deserts in Africa.

4. _____ hills in my town.

5. _____ a river near us.

6. _____ fish in the sea.

7. _____ mountains all around us.

8. _____ a lake in the valley.

9. _____ clouds in the sky.

B Look at the words in the box. Write questions about your classroom. Then answer the questions.

whiteboard	chairs	table	windows	posters on the walls
desks	teacher's desk	computers	bookshelves	TV

1. _Is there a whiteboard in the room?_
   Yes. There are two whiteboards in the room.

2. _____

3. _____

4. _____

5. _____

6. _____

7. _____

8. _____

C Write about the town or city you live in now and your hometown. Make affirmative and negative statements with *there is/was* and *there are/were*.

Town:	Hometown:
1. There is a sports stadium.	1. There wasn't a sports stadium.
2.	2.
3.	3.
4.	4.
5.	5.
6.	6.
7.	7.

Putting It Together

■ GRAMMAR

A Rewrite the sentences with mistakes. If there are no mistakes, write "C."

1. There were a lot of traffic yesterday.   _There was a lot of traffic yesterday._

2. There snow was on the mountains?   _____

3. I live far from a shopping mall.   _____

4. The forest was near to the lake.   _____

5. The children are in the beach.   _____

6. Many years ago there is just one continent.   _____

7. Now there's seven continents.   _____

8. In the photos you can see the beautiful valley.   _____

9. There were'nt any dolphins in the bay this morning.   _____

    _____

10. Were there fish in the sea?   _____

11. We were at a hotel at the mountains.   _____

B Circle the correct words to complete the e-mail.

Hi Mario:

I'm back from Belize. The trip was great. We were (1) in / on three different places: Mountain Pine Ridge Reserve, Belize City, and Dangriga. Mountain Pine Ridge Reserve is a pine forest (2) in / above a tropical forest. We stayed (3) on / at a resort (4) from / in the mountains. There are a lot of things to do in and around the reserve. There (5) is / are many waterfalls and small pools to see and swim in. (6) There is / There are one large waterfall called Thousand Foot Falls. It's beautiful! There are also caves (7) around / between the reserve. There is a cave (8) near / behind the river Rio Frio. It's very big! Caracol, the large ancient Mayan city, is (9) near / far from the reserve—only 33 miles away. We (10) was / were at Caracol for a whole day!

I'll tell you more about my trip tomorrow in class!

Ahmed

Find the words in the puzzle below and circle them.

```
L  N  R  W  A  F  C  V  N  I  S  O  X  Q  T
L  L  P  T  F  U  O  M  S  N  T  D  B  N  B
L  O  A  Z  I  L  Z  L  T  R  E  S  E  D  W
A  S  Z  F  C  U  A (Y  A  B) R  Y  K  K  A
K  L  E  A  R  N  P  H  K  N  X  Z  P  E  M
E  Y  N  A  D  E  M  O  U  N  T  A  I  N  R
A  O  N  S  B  U  T  F  O  R  E  S  T  I  H
Y  E  L  L  A  V  C  A  L  X  J  C  V  I  O
K  N  Z  G  L  K  R  D  W  E  F  E  L  L  R
J  P  R  B  L  Z  T  I  H  R  R  L  I  W  X
J  V  X  P  B  X  O  F  V  S  S  T  W  K  Y
W  O  I  E  F  M  A  W  Y  E  R  B  F  D  N
P  Q  T  H  U  V  F  C  W  H  A  K  C  Q  K
G  V  X  H  U  E  H  E  B  M  Y  T  C  L  D
F  Z  G  Q  F  O  Z  L  Z  A  L  N  N  E  Z
```

BAY

DESERT

FOREST

HILLS

ISLANDS

LAKE

MOUNTAIN

RIVER

SEA

VALLEY

VOLCANO

WATERFALL

The Simple Present Tense: Statements and Yes/No Questions; The Simple Present Tense: Information Questions

PART ONE   The Simple Present Tense: Statements and *Yes/No* Questions

A Complete each sentence with the correct form of the verb in parentheses.

1. That company (manufacture) _____manufactures_____ furniture.

2. My history professor (hate) _____ globalization.

3. I (want) _____ to talk to customer service.

4. Customer service (talk) _____ to customers online.

5. My boss (work) _____ in the head office in Seattle.

6. I (understand) _____ French.

7. Our employees (go) _____ to work early in the morning.

8. Jose (get) _____ a new car every year.

9. We (exercise) _____ every day.

10. She (live) _____ in Canada.

11. They (like) _____ their jobs in the factory.

12. He (own) _____ two houses and two cars.

B Change the affirmative sentences to the negative. Use contractions where possible.

1. I work every day.   _____I don't work every day._____

2. She gets up early in the morning. _____

3. We live in the city. _____

4. My parents think sports are important. _____

5. They come from Chile. _____

6. I understand your problem. _____

7. We want to go to the meeting. _____

8. They get good wages. _____

9. She hates her old car. _____

10. Mr. Perez uses the Internet at home. _____

11. Flo Co manufactures computer parts. _____

12. I like my office. _____

C **Write questions using the phrases in parentheses. Complete the short answers to the questions.**

1. (you work in a factory) _____ *Do you work in a factory?* _____

   Yes, _____ *I do.* _____

2. (she like her job) _____

   No, _____

3. (you read every day) _____

   No, _____

4. (they like globalization) _____

   Yes, _____

5. (he live in an apartment) _____

   Yes, _____

6. (you understand Spanish) _____

   Yes, _____

A Complete the questions with an appropriate information word from the box. Then match the questions to the answers.

| what | why | how many | who | where |

1. __Why__ do you like your job?   a. 50.

2. _____ buys your products?   b. I'm a customer service representative.

3. _____ computer technicians   c. India.
   work for you?

4. _____ do you do?   d. Computer stores in the United States.

5. _____ do you outsource jobs to?   e. It's really interesting.

B Write questions for the answers. Use the words in parentheses.

1. Q: (where / work) _____ Where do you work? _____

   A: In the bookstore.

2. Q: (what / do) _____

   A: I'm a cashier.

3. Q: (how many / work) _____

   A: I work five days a week.

4. Q: (why / work) _____

   A: I like books.

5. Q: (who / make) _____

   A: Joe's Pizzeria makes great pizza.

6. Q: (where / get) _____

   A: I get gas at the station on Maple Street.

7. Q: (how many / have) _____

   A: This town has two supermarkets.

8. Q: (why / walk to work) _____

   A: I walk to work because I like to exercise.

9. Q: (what / do) _____

   A: My family goes to church on Sundays.

10. Q: (who / drive) _____

    A: My wife drives the children to school.

11. Q: (when / go shopping) _____

    A: We go shopping on Saturdays.

C Write questions with the words in parentheses. Don't answer the questions.

1. (who / buy) _____ *Who buys computers from India?* _____

2. (who / have) _____

3. (who / works) _____

4. (what / happens) _____

5. (what / produces) _____

Putting It Together

■ GRAMMAR

A Complete the conversations.

1. Juan: What company _____ (you / work) for, Krissi?

   Krissi: For MicroLumen.

   Juan: How many employees _____ (the company / have)?

   Krissi: Fifty.

   Juan: What _____ (the company / manufacture)?

   Krissi: Plastic tubing for medical use.

   Juan: _____ (they / outsource)?

Krissi: No, _____ .

Juan: _____ (they / make a profit)?

Krissi: I _____ (not know).

Juan: Who _____ (buys) their products?

Krissi: Medical supply companies.

2. Ali: Where _____ (you / study English), Cho?

Cho: City Community College.

Ali: _____ (you / like) it?

Cho: Yes, _____ .

Ali: How many classes _____ (you / have)?

Cho: Two.

Ali: When _____ (you / have) class?

Cho: On Tuesdays and Thursdays.

Ali: Why _____ (you / take) two classes?

Cho: One is a conversation class and the other is a grammar class.

Ali: Which class _____ (you / like) more?

Cho: I like the conversation class more.

Unscramble each of the clue words. Use the numbered letters to complete the sentence below.

SOBS

14			

EPLEYMEO

			23	5		

NOIGATILLZAIBO

18	19		21	2		24	25	13	9	10	28	29

MARNAGE

		26	11	22		

FYRCAOT

			3		6	

RAFNUTMUCEA

		8				17	16			

ROEDR

15		4		

WEKROR

1	20		12		

SESTRO

27	7				

	H								H								
1		2	3	4	5	6	7	8	9	10	11	12	13	14	15	16	17

											?
18	19	20	21	22	23	24	25	26	27	10	28	29

Adverbs of Frequency;
Prepositions of Time

PART ONE	Adverbs of Frequency

A Unscramble the words to write sentences.

1. usually / shake hands / Americans

   Americans usually shake hands.

2. Latinos / on the cheek / kiss / often

   _____

3. touch / frequently / Americans / during conversation

   _____

4. smiles / my boss / rarely

   _____

5. retire / almost always / Americans / at 65

   _____

6. in public / kiss / in some cultures / people / never

   _____

7. calls / strangers / my mother / almost never / by their first names

   _____

8. say / always / my children / thank you and you're welcome

   _____

9. Americans / at 18 / get married / seldom

   _____

B Write about customs in your country. Use the adverb of frequency.

1. always   _We always have soup at the end of dinner._

2. usually   _____

3. occasionally   _____

4. rarely   _____

5. never   _____

PART TWO	Prepositions of Time

A Circle the correct preposition of time.

1. I work (from) / at 10:00 to 3:00 every day.

2. My wife gets home on / by 6:00 on weekdays.

3. Americans almost never retire before / after age 60.

4. I want to get up from / at 7:30.

5. At / In night we often watch a movie.

6. I rarely get ready on / in 30 minutes.

7. In / On Saturday there's a party at my house.

8. Babies usually begin to talk in / before age two.

B Answer these questions using prepositions of time.

1. When do you usually wake up?

     I usually wake up at 6:00 a.m.

2. What do you do after you wake up?

     _____

3. What time do you leave for work?

     _____

4. What time do you leave for class?

     _____

5. What time do you get home?

   _____

6. What do you do in the evenings?

   _____

7. What do you do on the weekends?

   _____

8. When do you do housework?

   _____

9. When do you do homework?

   _____

Putting It Together

■ GRAMMAR

A Complete the conversations with words from the box. Use each word once.

1.

sometimes	often	usually	in	always

Raul: When is your birthday?

Mei: _____*In*_____ April.

Raul: Do you _____ have a big party?

Mei: Never.

Raul: What do you do?

Mei: _____ we have a small party. We _____ just go to a nice restaurant.

Raul: That's what we _____ do.

2.

| almost always | on | occasionally | never | in the morning |

Rula: Do you like to exercise?

Holly: Yes.

Rula: When do you do it?

Holly: _____ Tuesdays, Thursdays, and Saturdays.

Rula: What do you do?

Holly: I _____ walk. _____ I ride a bike.

Rula: Do you go to a gym?

Holly: I _____ go to a gym.

Rula: I go to the gym everyday_____ .

■ VOCABULARY

Unscramble each of the clue words. Use the numbered letters to complete the sentence below.

SILME

| | | | | |
| 12 | | 10 | 4 | |

COHUT

| | | | | |
| 14 | 11 | 8 | 7 | 16 |

GKHIANS HASDN

| | | | | | | | | | | |
| | 13 | | 1 | | | | 3 | | | 22 |

SKSI

| | | | |
| | 6 | | |

TERREI

| | | | | | |
| 20 | 21 | 15 | 9 | 17 | |

TGE RIMRADE

| | | | | | | | | |
| | 19 | | | 2 | 5 | | 18 | |

| | ' | | | W | Y | | | | | | | | | | B | | |
| 1 | | 2 | 3 | 4 | 5 | 6 | 7 | 8 | 9 | 10 | 11 | 8 | 12 | 13 | | 11 | 8 | 14 |

| | | | | | | | | | | | | |
| 7 | 8 | 4 | 19 | 8 | 20 | 21 | 22 | | 11 | 15 | 16 | 17 | 18 |

Possessive Nouns; Possessive Adjectives; Possessive Pronouns; Questions with *Whose*

PART ONE	Possessive Nouns

A Write statements with possessive nouns using the words below.

1. Lars / car / new

   Lars' car is new.

2. Jane / sister / fifteen

   _____

3. Karen / parents / names / Judy and Roger

   _____

4. The children / school / in the city

   _____

5. Mr. Roberds / family / big

   _____

6. I / at / my uncle / house

   _____

7. The dogs / beds / on the floor

   _____

8. My sister / friends / children / in college

   _____

9. Thomas / house / next to my house

   _____

10. Carina and Joe / anniversary / on Monday

    _____

B Write the names of your family in the spaces below. Then write ten sentences that explain their relationships.

Grandparents _____

Parents _____

Brothers _____ Peter _____

Sisters _____

Uncles _____

Aunts _____

In-laws _____ Ann _____

Cousins _____

Daughters _____

Sons _____

Nieces _____

Nephews _____

1. _____ Ann is Peter's wife. _____

2. _____

3. _____

4. _____

5. _____

6. _____

7. _____

8. _____

9. _____

10. _____

A **Fill in the blanks with the possessive adjective.**

1. She takes _____ her _____ lunch to work every day.

2. I walk _____ dog three times a day.

3. My son puts _____ shoes on now.

4. We want to take _____ vacation in December.

5. The children love _____ parents very much.

6. You can wash _____ clothes in our machine.

7. He cleans _____ car once a month.

8. Our neighbors take good care of _____ yard.

9. A baby needs _____ mother.

10. My sister's fish are _____ favorite hobby.

11. Americans usually clean _____ own homes.

12. Some employers give bonuses to _____ employees.

B **Circle the correct word.**

1. (I / (My)) father's family lives in (we / our) town.

2. (They / Their) come to (I / my) house every day.

3. (We / Our) house is next to (they / their) house.

4. (He / His) family is more important to him than (he / his) job.

5. (You / Your) friend called from (he / his) cell phone.

6. (It / Its) is an incredible machine, the computer; (it / its) applications are endless.

7. (You / your) are late to class. (You / Your) teacher already closed the door.

8. (I / my) usually do (I / my) homework in the evening.

9. (She / Her) really likes (she / her) new job.

10. (Its / It's) a strange animal; (it's / its) called a capybara.

11. (We / Our) want to go camping with (we / our) friends.

12. (They / Their) dog sleeps in (they / their) garage.

C **Rewrite the sentences. Use possessive pronouns and/or *whose*.**

1. Your family is traditional. My family is blended.

   Yours is traditional. Mine is blended.

2. My apartment is big. Your apartment is small.

3. His father is 54. Her father is 62.

4. Our family is large. Their family is small.

5. Their children are grown up. Our children are young.

6. Whose books are those? Whose books are these?

7. Are you sure this is our classroom? Yes, it's our classroom.

8. Your idea was good. My idea wasn't good.

9. Her wedding was at night. My wedding was in the afternoon.

10. Her family is from Puerto Rico. His family isn't from Puerto Rico.

11. This is your telephone. That's my telephone.

12. Your family is on vacation. Their family isn't on vacation.

Putting It Together

A Soon-yi and Eve are looking at family pictures. Complete the conversation with the correct word. Use the subject pronoun in parentheses, or a possessive adjective, possessive pronoun, or possessive noun.

Soon-yi: Wow, (you) _____*you*_____ have a big family! (I) _____*Mine*_____ isn't very big.

Eve: (I) _____ is big because it's a blended family.

Soon-yi: Oh! Who's this?

Eve: My half sister, Dora. (We) _____ have different fathers: this is (I) _____ and this is (Dora) _____ .

Soon-yi: What about (you) _____ mother?

Eve: (We) _____ have the same mother.

Soon-yi: And what about (you) _____ brother, Mica?

Eve: He's my stepbrother. (He) _____ father is my stepfather. (He) _____ mother isn't (I) _____ .

Soon-yi: Whose brother and sister are they?

Eve: They're (I) _____ !

Soon-yi: So there are five children in (you) _____ blended family.

Eve: Yes. And these are (I) _____ grandparents, and those are (they) _____ .

Soon-yi: Enough! It's too complicated.

Find the words in the puzzle below and circle them.

```
H  J  Y  F  C  K  U  M  V  R  D  P  R  R  L
F  A  Z  L  X  E  F  T  S  X  A  V  E  T  A
N  Q  L  H  I  P  J  P  T  R  J  H  T  Y  V
X  M  O  F  H  M  D  I  E  N  T  E  S  J  C
J  T  O  A  B  D  A  N  P  A  Q  J  I  P  U
X  A  I  Q  L  R  T  F  F  P  L  G  S  H  J
G  M  Q  I  Y  S  O  L  A  O  J  L  G  M  V
D  E  D  N  E  L  B  T  T  V  G  G  C  H  A
U  S  S  E  J  F  U  M  H  Y  Z  D  S  U  J
N  B  I  A  W  K  M  E  E  M  H  V  T  R
M  O  T  H  E  R  L  K  R  Y  R  K  O  P  C
H  D  D  W  C  T  Q  M  X  M  G  T  E  O  J
K  G  R  A  N  D  P  A  R  E  N  T  S  Q  N
Y  O  M  D  W  T  B  A  O  X  M  K  T  P  S
W  W  U  W  U  G  L  Q  P  W  V  C  P  C  S
```

BLENDED

FAMILY

FATHER

GRANDPARENTS

HALFBROTHER

MOTHER

PARENTS

SISTER

STEPFATHER

Personal Pronouns;
One, Ones, It, Them/They

PART ONE	Personal Pronouns

A **Fill in the blank with the object pronoun. Underline the noun it is replacing.**

1. I love these <u>plates!</u> I want to buy _____*them*_____ .

2. We're having chicken for dinner. My family likes _____ a lot.

3. I bought a new car. I parked _____ in the garage.

4. The children are tired. We played with _____ in the morning.

5. The price of gas is high. They raised _____ again today.

6. Where's her car? She sold _____ yesterday.

7. I don't know where Selena is. I called _____ five times today.

8. These new boots are beautiful. Alexandra sells _____ in her shop.

9. I ordered some books online. They're going to ship _____ tomorrow.

10. This merchandise is really inexpensive. We import _____ from China.

11. We talk with our parents all the time. They called _____ last night.

12. I know Sandra very well. I work with _____ .

B **Unscramble the sentences.**

1. about / they / you / all the time / talk

    They talk about you all the time.

2. very much / love / them / I

_____

3. my / me / she / helps / with / homework

_____

4. call / I / him / once a day

_____

5. me / walk / they / with / usually

_____

6. below / they / in / apartment / the / me / live

_____

7. party / them / invited / we / our / to

_____

8. it / finish / me / please / help

_____

PART TWO   *One, Ones, It, Them/They*

A **Rewrite the sentence with *one, ones, it,* or *them/they.***

1. He has <u>a drink</u>.   _____ He has one. _____

2. She has <u>a hamburger</u>.   _____

3. They have yellow <u>flowers</u>.   _____

4. We have purple <u>flowers</u>.   _____

5. This is <u>the street</u>.   _____

6. That is <u>the restaurant</u>.   _____

7. Do you have <u>the merchandise</u>?   _____

8. Do you see <u>his house</u>?   _____

9. Please take <u>the samples</u>.   _____

10. Where did you see <u>the pictures</u>?   _____

11. Talk to <u>your mother's friends</u>.   _____

12. Stay with <u>your new friends</u>.   _____

B **Rewrite the sentences. Replace the underlined words with *one, ones, it,* or *them/ they.* Keep descriptive adjectives.**

1. I have a desk. I really like <u>the desk</u>. It's <u>a nice desk</u>.

   I have a desk. I really like it. It's a nice one.

2. He's taking an ESL class at college. He likes <u>the class.</u> It's a <u>good class.</u>

   _____

3. All of <u>the students</u> will be attending <u>the graduation party</u>.

   _____

4. I like hotels. <u>Hotels</u> are nice, but we don't usually stay in hotels on our vacation. However, we will stay in <u>a hotel</u> this time.

   _____

5. They don't have yellow roses, but they do have pink <u>roses</u> and red <u>roses</u>.

   _____

6. I saw an interesting bird last week, a rare <u>bird</u>, but <u>the bird</u> isn't here now.

   _____

7. Where did you put the pencils? I put <u>the pencils</u> on the shelf. <u>The pencils</u> are on the shelf in the kitchen.

   _____

Putting It Together

GRAMMAR

A **Complete the conversation. Use personal pronouns and *one, ones, it,* and *them/ they.***

Mark: I want to buy a new motorcycle.

Doug: Didn't you buy _____ last week?

Mark: Yes, but I don't like _____ . _____ is too slow. I want a fast _____ . I saw some great motorcycles at a new shop.

Doug: Are _____ expensive?

Mark: Yes, _____ are.

Doug: Do you have enough money for the new motorcycle?

Mark: Not really.

Doug: Then you shouldn't buy _____ .

Mark: But I'm going to sell my old _____ and buy a new

_____ .

Doug: Oh, OK.

B **Rewrite the sentences with mistakes. If there are no mistakes, write "C."**

1. Does she have a receipt? Yes, she has it. _____Yes, she has one._____

2. I talk to she every day. _____

3. He imports goods from China. _____

4. I don't like they house. _____

5. She bought the pretty ones. _____

6. Their so beautiful. _____

7. They spoke with you and he. _____

8. She wants this ones. _____

9. I'm going to work with she. _____

10. Do they want samples? Yes, they want it. _____

Complete the sentences. Then solve the puzzle.

Across

1. The successful company made a good _____.

4. He will _____ the antiques to New York.

5. The other company made a bad _____.

6. The price of corn will probably _____ in the future.

Down

1. What is the _____ of that car?

2. I _____ goods from China.

3. The price of gas will _____ higher in the future.

4. The supermarket _____ me food.

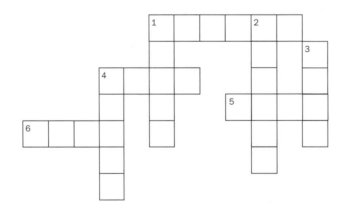

Lesson ⑧

The Present Progressive Tense: Statements, *Yes/No* Questions, Short Answers; The Present Progressive Tense: Information Questions

PART ONE	The Present Progressive Tense: Statements, *Yes/No* Questions, Short Answers

A Rewrite the sentences. Use the present progressive.

1. The satellite orbits Earth.

   The satellite is orbiting Earth.

2. Earth orbits the sun.

   _____

3. The sun shines.

   _____

4. Astronauts float in space.

   _____

5. The shuttle takes off.

   _____

6. The telescope works.

   _____

7. The planets orbit the sun.

   _____

8. The shuttle travels in space.

   _____

9. The moon shines at night.

   _____

10. Some say that aliens live on other planets.

    _____

B **Rewrite the sentences. Make them negative. Use contractions.**

1. I'm studying astronomy.

   _____ I'm not studying astronomy. _____

2. We're talking about space and the planets.

   _____

3. They're looking at the moon.

   _____

4. The astronauts are returning to Earth.

   _____

5. Aliens are invading Earth.

   _____

6. The satellite is sending images to the moon.

   _____

7. The sun is burning Earth.

   _____

8. I'm using a telescope to look at the moon.

   _____

C **Write *yes/no* questions in the present progressive. Then complete the short answers.**

1. you / go / to / class / now

   _____ Are you going to class now? _____

   Yes, _____ I am. _____

2. they / eat / in the cafeteria

   _____

   No, _____

3. he / study / the planets

   _____

   Yes, _____

4. she / call / her parents

   _____

   No, _____

5. you / work / on a project

   _____

   No, _____

D Describe what is happening around you. Use complete sentences.

1. _____ My brother is watching TV. _____

2. _____

3. _____

4. _____

5. _____

PART TWO **The Present Progressive Tense: Information Questions**

A Match the information questions with the answers. Draw a line.

1. What are you doing?   a. Matt is.

2. Why are you going?   b. By car.

3. Where are you going?   c. I'm going to the supermarket.

4. How are you going?   d. Because we need food.

5. Who is going with you?   e. I'm looking in the refrigerator.

B Write information questions for the answers. The underlined word or phrase is the answer. Use *who*, *what*, *where*, *why*, and *how*.

1. _____ What is John doing? _____

   John is <u>writing an e-mail</u>.

2. _____

   <u>Aliens</u> are invading Earth.

3. _____

   Professor Hill is <u>teaching an astronomy class</u>.

4. _____

   <u>The astronaut</u> is entering the shuttle.

5. _____

   We're going <u>home</u>.

6. _____

   They're going home <u>by bus</u>.

7. _____

   She's running to class <u>because she's late</u>.

8. _____

   We're studying <u>in the park</u>.

9. _____

He's <u>watching a TV program</u> about the planets.

10. _____

I'm looking at the sky <u>because it's cloudy</u>.

11. _____

<u>Hundreds of people</u> are using the SETI program.

12. _____

I'm looking at the planets <u>with a telescope</u>.

13. _____

The shuttle is traveling <u>to the space station</u>.

14. _____

<u>The students</u> are visiting the space center.

Putting It Together

■ GRAMMAR

A Complete the conversation. You may need to supply a question word.

Solin: Hi Juli. _____*What*_____ are you doing?

Juli: _____ (learn) about the planets.

Solin: _____ (learn) about them?

Juli: I'm watching a program on the Universe Channel.

Solin: _____ (watch) it right now?

Juli: Yes, _____ . Why?

Solin: I'm going out. Do you want to go with me?

Juli: Where _____ (go)?

Solin: _____ (go) outside to learn about the universe.

Juli: Huh?

Solin: The sun _____ (eclipse) the moon today!

Juli: Oh, I forgot. I'm coming!

B Rewrite the sentences with mistakes. If there are no mistakes, write "C."

1. I reading about a new planet   _____*I'm reading about a new planet.*_____

2. No, it isn't.   _____

3. It is orbiting our sun? _____

4. The weather is getting cool. _____

5. Yes, it's. _____

6. Where you going? _____

7. What's happening now? _____

8. How you are doing? _____

9. She's not looking for aliens. _____

10. How you looking for planets? _____

■ VOCABULARY

Use the clues to solve the puzzle.

Across

2. It shines at night.

4. our planet

6. They don't live on our planet.

7. an airplane for space

8. The planets are in this.

11. a person who flies to space

Down

1. You use it to look at the planets and stars.

3. to go around

5. It sends signals.

9. Mars is one of them.

10. It shines in the day.

The Present Progressive Tense vs. the Simple Present Tense; Stative Verbs

PART ONE   The Present Progressive Tense vs. the Simple Present Tense

A Complete the sentences with the correct form and tense of the verb in parentheses. Use the present progressive or the simple present.

1. In the United States, people _____*shake*_____ (shake) hands when they greet.

2. Factory X _____ (make) men's clothing.

3. Many animals _____ (live) in the forest.

4. We _____ (import) many products from China this year.

5. Our company always _____ (make) a profit.

6. Prices _____ (rise) right now.

7. They _____ (sell) used cars.

8. Earth _____ (orbit) around the sun once a year.

9. The shuttle _____ (travel) to the space station this year.

10. The editors _____ (have) a meeting in room 8B.

B Imagine you're camping by a lake. Write five facts about the campground. Then write five actions that are happening right now at the campground.

Five facts about the campground	Five actions happening now at the campground
The campground has a lot of trees.	He's cutting down a tree.

A **Choose the correct form of the verb for each sentence.**

1. That perfume (smells / is smelling) nice.

2. I (think / am thinking) about my homework for tomorrow.

3. We (hear / are hearing) a lot of bad comments about the Web site.

4. The tea (tastes / is tasting) bitter.

5. I (don't feel excited / am not feeling excited) about my new classes right away.

6. He (has / is having) a large boat.

7. They (don't see / are not seeing) the stop sign.

8. I (smell / am smelling) the milk to see if it's fresh.

9. We (have / are having) a great day.

10. She (thinks / is thinking) we spend too much money.

11. We (see / are seeing) a lot of car accidents on our street recently.

12. I (feel / am feeling) that animal rights are important.

13. I (don't hear / am not hearing) you well; the batteries are low.

B **Write a sentence in the simple present and present progressive for each word in parentheses.**

1. (think) _____

_____

2. (feel) _____

_____

3. (have) _____

_____

4. (see) _____

_____

Putting It Together

GRAMMAR

A Complete the conversation. Use the correct tense of the verb in parentheses.

Jasmin: Hi Simon. What are you doing?

Simon: I _____*am reading*_____ (read) about the gypsy moth.

Jasmin: What is the gypsy moth?

Simon: The gypsy moth is an insect. When gypsy moths are caterpillars, they _____ (eat) the leaves off trees.

Jasmin: Lots of bugs _____ (eat) leaves.

Simon: The gypsy moth caterpillars _____ (damage) forests. They can deforest large areas quickly. They _____ (make) the trees vulnerable to disease. They can kill trees.

Jasmin: Wow! I _____ (not know) about this!

Simon: Right now the caterpillars _____ (infest) large forests in the north and northeast. They _____ (eat) all the trees. And they _____ (move) west and south.

Simon: Oh, no!

Jasmin: States in the west and the east _____ (prepare) to fight the caterpillars.

Simon: What are they doing?

Jasmin: They're _____ (educate) the public. Also, they're _____ (train) the tourism industry. No forests, no tourists!

Simon: _____ (think) they can save the forests!

Jasmin: I _____ (think) they can save a lot of the forests, but not all of them. This is a big problem.

B Rewrite the sentences with mistakes. If there are no mistakes, write "C."

1. They're having a new dog. _____*They have a new dog.*_____

2. I smelling something strange. _____

3. I'm seeing a smile on your face. _____

4. She walks to school right now. _____

5. Caterpillars are eating leaves in the summer. _____

6. He work for the U.S. Coast Guard. _____

7. I'm thinking we can buy a new house. _____

8. I smell the coffee. _____

9. We have a lot of pollution. _____

10. Rangers protecting the forests. _____

■ VOCABULARY

Unscramble each of the clue words. Use the numbered letters to complete the sentence at the bottom.

REET   □□□□
          6

BRCAHN   □□□□□□
              5

FAEL   □□□□
     10 2

SIDSAEE   □□□□□□□
      1

LOILONPUT   □□□□□□□□□

GOGRSLE   □□□□□□□
        3   11

PERSTTORSE   □□□□□□□□□□
       4

CEPROTT   □□□□□□□
   8

RARENG   □□□□□□
        9

TUC WOND   □□□ □□□□□
      7

□ □(V) □   □□□   □□□□□ !
1 2 3   4 5 6   7 8 9 10 11

Time Sequence Markers; Prepositions of Movement

PART ONE	Time Sequence Markers

A Below are the steps to make an apple pie. Put the steps in order, numbering them from 1 to 11.

1. ___ Put the apple filling into the pie crust.

2. ___ Cover the pie with the other piece of crust.

3. ___ Peel and slice the apples.

4. ___ Cut small vents in the top crust.

5. _1_ Buy two pieces of ready-made pie crust, apples, flour, sugar, lemon juice, cinnamon, and salt.

6. ___ Put one pie crust into a pie pan.

7. ___ Put pieces of butter on top of the apple filling.

8. ___ Preheat oven to 400 degrees.

9. ___ Bake for 40–50 minutes.

10. ___ Mix apples lightly with flour, sugar, lemon juice, cinnamon, and salt.

11. ___ Squeeze the edges of the top and bottom crust together.

B Use time sequence markers to write the steps from exercise A.

First, buy two pieces of ready-made pie crust, apples, flour, sugar, lemon juice, cinnamon, and salt.

C Below are the steps to send a fax. Put the steps in order, numbering them from 1 to 6.

1. _1_ Prepare a cover sheet with information about the sender and the receiver.

2. ___ Wait for the machine to send each document.

3. ___ Dial the number to where the fax is going.

4. ___ When you receive a fax signal, press send.

5. ___ Place all documents to be faxed face up in the fax tray.

6. ___ When finished, the fax machine will say, "Fax Complete."

D Create a conversation between Jose and Frank. Jose wants to learn how to send a fax. Use the steps in exercise C and time sequence markers.

Jose: Frank, I need to send a fax.

Frank: _First, prepare a cover sheet with information about the sender and the receiver._

Jose: _____

Frank: _____

Jose: _____

Frank: _____

Jose: _____

Frank: _____

Jose: _____

Frank: _____

Jose: _____

Frank: _____

Jose: Thanks, Frank!

A Circle the simple preposition or the preposition of movement in the following sentences.

1. They're walking (out / (out of)) the train station.

2. The train stopped. Mary is getting (off / off of).

3. The photocopier glass was clean. She placed the paper (on / onto) it.

4. The cat jumped (on / onto) the table.

5. The taxi stopped and a person came (out / out of).

6. She got to the door and walked (in / into).

7. The pencil rolled (off / off of) the desk.

8. We ran (in / into) the room.

B Circle the correct preposition.

1. They're walking (onto / (toward)) the train station.

2. The team is climbing (by / up) the mountain.

3. He's running (along / through) the bank of the river.

4. She's jogging (through / down) five flights of stairs.

5. They're arriving (through / off of) the door.

6. The birds are flying (past / into) mountains.

7. We're driving quickly (into / by) shops and restaurants.

8. They're walking (by / into) the large supermarket and going into the small shops.

9. Are you going (into / along) the library now?

10. The man is driving (out of / off of) the garage and onto the street.

11. The police officer is falling (down / off of) his horse!

12. The puppy is climbing (through / onto) the sofa.

GRAMMAR

A Complete the conversation with a time sequence marker from the box. (Answers may vary.)

first	then	finally	after that	next

Mike: Hey, Lily. What are you doing?

Lily: I'm editing a video.

Mike: How do you do it?

Lily: _____*First*_____ , I upload all of the images from the camera onto the computer.

Mike: Then what?

Lily: _____ I select parts of the video I need to create my story.

Mike: OK, what next?

Lily: _____ I put the parts together.

Mike: And what else?

Lily: _____ , I add special effects like fades and dissolves.

Mike: What else do you do?

Lily: I add titles and credits. And _____ , I add music.

Mike: That's a lot of work!

Lily: Yeah, but it's fun.

B Complete the letter with a word from the box.

through	into	finally	onto	first
along	toward	next	after that	down

Dear Mom:

I'm having a lot of fun at college. I'm very busy, but I love it. _*first*_ , I get up and go running _____ the river. _____ I run _____ downtown. When I get to Broadway, I go _____ the tunnel and _____ the subway station. _____ I hop _____ a train and go back to the dormitory. _____ , I go _____ the hill to the cafeteria to eat breakfast and get ready to start my busy day.

Love,
Carolina

Find the words in the puzzle below and circle them.

```
R  S  A  P  A  K  S  I  L  D  Z  A  P  N  Z
E  A  S  X  T  C  S  K  D  K  B  V  X  B  N
I  O  K  A  R  M  S  H  J  B  S  S  Z  O  M
P  W  P  E  L  E  E  V  N  Q  L  B  C  S  L
O  J  E  N  U  G  O  E  F  A  X  M  R  T  V
C  N  K  X  Q  C  F  J  T  E  W  R  E  N  R
O  O  Y  X  X  D  F  Y  D  I  O  D  V  Z  W
T  A  M  A  C  H  I  N  E  D  N  T  O  R  M
O  J  B  V  D  L  C  H  I  F  T  G  C  G  Y
H  Z  L  S  I  X  E  R  N  O  T  T  U  B  Y
P  N  C  H  T  M  R  P  X  X  E  O  W  B  V
U  I  C  O  B  O  K  H  W  U  M  R  N  I  F
B  P  T  C  C  H  U  U  M  E  V  J  V  I  S
S  D  W  Y  J  E  Q  Y  M  R  M  I  J  H  H
G  A  H  S  Y  G  G  J  V  I  T  R  O  K  D
```

BUTTON

CORRIDOR

COVER

FAX

GLASS

MACHINE

MEETING

MEMO

OFFICE

PHOTOCOPIER

SCREEN

I. Paragraph Form

A Read the notes about forming a paragraph.

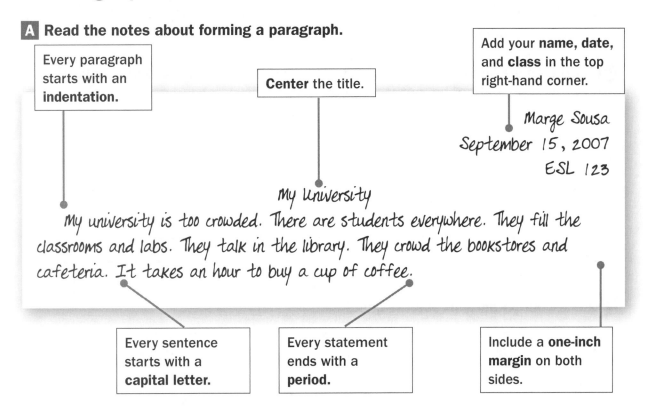

Every paragraph starts with an **indentation**.

Center the title.

Add your **name, date,** and **class** in the top right-hand corner.

Marge Sousa
September 15, 2007
ESL 123

My University

My university is too crowded. There are students everywhere. They fill the classrooms and labs. They talk in the library. They crowd the bookstores and cafeteria. It takes an hour to buy a cup of coffee.

Every sentence starts with a **capital letter.**

Every statement ends with a **period.**

Include a **one-inch margin** on both sides.

II. Punctuation Review

B Look at Appendices 7 and 8 in the student book (page 247). Use the punctuation and capitalization rules to correct the following sentences.

Kim

1. ~~kim~~ ^ works in a factory.

2. The Ottoman Empire was in north Africa.

3. Was it raining yesterday.

4. Pangaea was a continent three hundred million years ago

5. EnormoCorp makes computers, printers, and fax machines.

6. Basia is russian.

7. Oh no. The factory is closed.

III. Writing a Descriptive Paragraph

Look at the paragraph in the Grammar and Vocabulary feature on page 48 of your student book. This is a **descriptive paragraph.** A descriptive paragraph gives a picture of a person, place, thing, or idea. It shows how the subject looks, smells, tastes, sounds, and/or feels.

C Use the space below to write a paragraph using the Grammar and Vocabulary feature on page 48 of your student book.

| |
| |
| |
| |
| |
| |

D Check your paragraph. Use the checklist.

	Yes	No
Indentation		
Capital letters to start sentences		
Periods at the end of sentences		
Name, date, class		
Title centered		
Grammar from lessons 1–10		

E Rewrite your paragraph.

| |
| |
| |
| |
| |
| |

General Statements: Ø and *A/An*; General and Specific Statements: Ø and *The*

PART ONE	General Statements: Ø and *A/An*

A Check the correct sentences.

1. ✓ I love a rainy day.

2. ___ A king ruled England for centuries.

3. ___ A rice is the most important grain in the world.

4. ___ Islands are created when volcanoes erupt.

5. ___ Many Americans aren't happy with a globalization.

6. ___ Customer service is an important part of a business.

7. ___ Aliens live on other planets.

8. ___ Satellites orbit Earth.

9. ___ A pollution causes health problems.

10. ___ It's good to have meeting once in a while.

B Complete the sentences with *a/an* or Ø.

1. __A__ cat is a better pet than __a__ dog.

2. _____ veterinarian earns _____ high salary.

3. _____ tag sale is _____ good place for buying _____ appliances.

4. _____ students study _____ math and _____ English in _____ college.

5. _____ flowers are _____ nice gift.

6. _____ rose is _____ beautiful flower.

7. I like to swim in _____ lakes better than in _____ swimming pools.

8. People use _____ microwaves too much.

9. It was _____ great movie. I like movies about _____ real events.

10. _____ Internet dating is _____ great way to meet _____ people.

A Label the statements *general* or *specific*. Then change the general statements to specific statements, and the specific statements to general statements. Use *the* or Ø. (Answers will vary.)

1. Pets demand a lot of attention. _____ *general* _____
   _____ The pets in our house demand a lot of attention. _____

2. People do not elect queens. _____
   _____

3. The artists in our community don't make a lot of money. _____
   _____

4. The doctors in our hospital are very smart. _____
   _____

5. Volcanoes erupt without warning. _____
   _____

6. Forests have a lot of wildlife. _____
   _____

7. Workers often belong to a union. _____
   _____

8. They bought factories. _____
   _____

B Complete the sentences with *the* or Ø.

1. I like taking __Ø__ night classes.

2. I like _____ night classes in our school.

3. _____ weather reports are not always accurate.

4. Every morning I listen to _____ weather report on the radio.

5. _____ animals in zoos can often become bored and depressed.

6. _____ animals in the Belize Zoo live in a very natural habitat.

7. We go to _____ new restaurants every month.

8. _____ restaurants in our town are fantastic.

9. _____ families are very important in Latin America.

10. _____ family came over to our house for Christmas.

Putting It Together

■ GRAMMAR

A Complete the sentences with *a/an*, *the*, or Ø.

1. I'm taking ___*a*___ trip to Alaska next year. _____ trip is going to last three weeks.

2. There are two umbrellas: _____ big one and _____ small one. Do you want _____ big one?

3. _____ goldfish make wonderful pets for children. My students love _____ fish in our classroom.

4. Today we bought _____ new computer and _____ printer. _____ computer is on my desk, but _____ printer is still in _____ box.

5. _____ fish make great _____ pets.

6. I called customer service and asked to speak to _____ representative. _____ representative helped me receive a refund.

7. We have _____ minivan and _____ jeep. We're going to use _____ jeep today.

8. _____ soccer is _____ great sport.

9. Would you like_____ appetizer and _____ drink? _____ drinks are at the bar and _____ appetizers are on the table.

10. _____ dormitories are a great place for new college students to live.

11. We live in _____ house in _____ city of New Haven.

12. _____ students in my class are from _____ different countries.

13. _____ vacation resorts like Club Med and Sandals are good for families with young children.

14. I read _____ book. _____ book was about _____ family who was shipwrecked on a desert island. _____ family was from Canada. _____ island was in the Pacific.

15. I packed my son _____ lunch this morning. I gave him _____ apple, _____ sandwich, and _____ milk.

16. Did you find _____ person you were looking for on the Internet?

17. She found _____ wallet in the street.

■ VOCABULARY

Unscramble each of the clue words. Use the numbered letters to complete the sentence at the bottom.

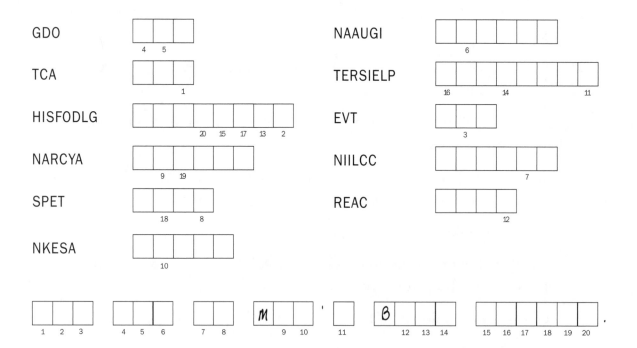

GDO ☐☐☐
     4 5

TCA ☐☐☐
      1

HISFODLG ☐☐☐☐☐☐☐☐
          20 15 17 13 2

NARCYA ☐☐☐☐☐☐
        9 19

SPET ☐☐☐☐
     18 8

NKESA ☐☐☐☐☐
        10

NAAUGI ☐☐☐☐☐☐
           6

TERSIELP ☐☐☐☐☐☐☐☐
          16   14   11

EVT ☐☐☐
     3

NIILCC ☐☐☐☐☐☐
            7

REAC ☐☐☐☐
       12

☐☐☐ ☐☐☐ ☐☐☐ M☐☐ ' ☐ B☐☐☐ ☐☐☐☐☐☐ .
1 2 3 4 5 6 7 8   9 10 11 12 13 14 15 16 17 18 19 20

Quantifiers; Quantifiers with *Too*

Quantifiers

A **Circle the correct quantifier.**

1. We don't get (**much** / many) rain in Arizona.

2. There were (few / some) clouds today; it was nice and sunny.

3. I don't know (any / some) world history.

4. There are (a lot of / a little) islands in the South Pacific.

5. There are (any / a few) deserts in the United States.

6. There's (much / a lot of) good bacteria in yogurt.

7. There is (little / some) pollution in my town; the air is clean and safe.

8. There isn't (much / many) heart disease among women in Japan.

9. (Some / few) globalization is good for everyone.

10. I take (a few / much) vitamins every day.

11. There's (a lot of / a few) protein in eggs.

12. (Much / Many) Americans get married at a late age.

13. (A little / Little) amount of fat in your diet is good.

14. (Few / A few) American families today have more than three children.

B **Write nine sentences using the quantifiers in the box. Use each quantifier only once.**

a lot of	a little	many	some	any
much	little	a few	few	

1. _____ I drink a lot of water. _____

2. _____

3. _____

4. _____

5. _____

6. _____

7. _____

8. _____

9. _____

10. _____

PART TWO   **Quantifiers with *Too***

A Complete the sentences with the correct quantifier: *too much/too many; too few/ too little.*

1. There's ____*too much*____ food on my plate. I can't finish.

2. Americans eat too much sugar and _____ fresh fruit.

3. _____ sun is bad for your skin.

4. There's _____ pollution in Mexico City.

5. _____ Americans learn a second language.

6. Six months is _____ time to train for a marathon.

7. There's _____ evidence to suggest that aliens exist.

8. There are _____ stars in the universe to count.

9. There are _____ rangers to protect our large number of parks.

10. _____ bacteria in a cut can cause an infection.

B Write a true sentence about you or someone you know using the ideas and quantifiers in parentheses.

1. (exercise / too little)

_____

2. (vegetables / too few)

_____

3. (time / too much)

_____

4. (animals / too many)

_____

Putting It Together

■ GRAMMAR

A Complete the e-mail with the quantifiers from the box. Answers may vary. Some quantifiers may be used more than once.

a lot of	a little	many	some	any	too much	too little
much	little	a few	few	too many	too few	

Hi Mom,

We just got back from Peru! I had _a lot of_ fun and I made _____ new friends. _____ students from my class were on the trip; most of them were from other classes. And _____ people, about five, were from other schools.

Peru is amazing! We were very busy—there was _____ time to get bored and _____ to do! We went to Machu Picchu, Lake Titicaca, and the Sacred Valley. We did a lot, but there was _____ time to see everything. There were _____ things we wanted to do, but couldn't. For example, there wasn't _____ time to go to the Amazon. And we only saw _____ of Lima. It's a big city. Also, we didn't do _____ shopping. In my opinion, we went to _____ museums and _____ stores. However, we had _____ time at the airport and I was able to buy _____ souvenirs.

I can't wait to see you next month. I'll tell you all about Peru then.
Love,
Alex

B Rewrite the sentences with mistakes. If there are no mistakes, write "C."

1. She has a lot cats in her apartment. _____ She has a lot of cats in her apartment._____

2. There wasn't any time to go out. _____

3. He has too little friends to have a party.

_____

4. There's too much noise in here.

_____

5. American women couldn't vote few decades ago.

_____

6. My mother has little patience with rude people.

_____

7. There isn't many sugar in this coffee.

_____

8. Please have some fruit.

_____

9. I need any help.

_____

10. I watched a few movies this weekend.

_____

■ VOCABULARY

Use the clues to solve the puzzle.

Across

2. Too much is not good.

4. It grows on trees.

6. iron and zinc are just two

8. the nutrition in food

Down

1. can cause infection

3. Red meat, chicken, and fish all contain a lot of this.

5. energy

7. When you exercise, you _____ .

Regular Comparative Adjectives; Irregular Comparative Adjectives

A Complete the sentences with the comparative form of the adjective in parentheses.

1. New York is _____more humid_____ (humid) than Arizona.

2. A plane _____ (fast) than a bus.

3. The afternoon is _____ (sunny) than the evening.

4. Our cat is _____ (gentle) than our dog.

5. Spanish speakers are _____ (common) than French speakers in the United States.

6. It's _____ (cold) in Canada than in Costa Rica.

7. Community colleges are _____ (expensive) than private colleges.

8. Spring is _____ (cool) than summer.

9. Skydiving is _____ (dangerous) than riding a bike.

10. Running five miles is _____ (difficult) than running a marathon.

11. A lake is _____ (big) than a pond.

12. A city is _____ (crowded) than a town.

B Complete the dialogues with the comparative form of the adjective in parentheses.

1. Raul: Do you like this apartment?

   Isabela: No. There aren't many windows. My apartment is _____brighter_____ (bright).

2. Nina: Do you like this car?

   Abel: No. It's too big. My car is _____ (fuel efficient).

61

3.   Andrea: Do you like dogs?

       Sam: No. I like cats. They're _____ (intelligent).

4.   Peter: Do you like your new job?

     Grace: Yes. It's more relaxing and _____ (stressful) than my other job.

5.   Jasmin: Do you like this pizza?

      Juan: No. My mother's is _____ (tasty).

6.   Avril: Do you like your classes this year?

      Liam: No. They're _____ (interesting) than last year's classes.

7.   Ali: Do you like your new iMac® computer?

Muhammed: Yes, it's _____ (simple) to use than a PC.

8.   Akeem: Do you like the food in the cafeteria?

      Jane: No, I don't. My cooking is _____ (healthy).

PART TWO   **Irregular Comparative Adjectives**

A Complete the sentences with the comparative form of the adjective in parentheses.

1. Organic food is _____*better*_____ (good) for you than nonorganic food.

2. Fast food usually has _____ (a lot of) calories than home-cooked food.

3. My stomachache is _____ (bad) today than it was yesterday.

4. Older people need _____ (a few) calories than young adults.

5. Their rock group doesn't need _____ (much) practice than ours.

6. I think organic food is _____ (good) than nonorganic food.

7. They live _____ (far) from the school than we do.

8. Not exercising is _____ (bad) than eating too much.

9. We need _____ (a few) shopping malls and more farms.

10. In my opinion _____ (a little) globalization is better than more globalization.

B Complete the sentences with the comparative form of an adjective from the box.
Use each adjective only once.

| good | bad | far | a few | a lot of | a little | much |

1. My friend Ann has _____ more _____ experience in baking than I do. She bakes every day.

2. Ana has a _____ dorm room than I do. It's prettier and bigger.

3. My mother has a _____ accent than I do. She started speaking English when she was 55.

4. Now that I run every day, I need _____ calories than I needed before.

5. My family lives _____ from the train station than your family.

6. The United States has _____ farms now than 50 years ago.

7. Individual citizens have _____ control over land development than corporations have.

Putting It Together

A Write the missing form of the adjective in the chart.

Adjective	Comparative
good	better
easy	
warm	
quiet	
	sadder
beautiful	
few	
	worse
happy	
	more serious
	less
a lot of	
big	
nice	

B Compare two friends or two members of your family. Use regular and irregular adjectives.

Name:	Name:
Tom is shorter than Angela.	Angela is taller than Tom.

Find the words in the puzzle below and circle them.

```
R  K  T  X  Q  Q  D  T  R  V  B  J  Z  Y  O
Q  E  E  W  W  X  R  C  B  L  O  M  L  Y  M
W  Z  M  O  D  A  E  H  C  R  O  P  S  J  C
X  H  H  R  C  V  L  I  H  B  Z  I  B  E  L
P  R  E  T  A  Y  T  C  A  K  U  T  T  Q  Y
E  E  O  A  E  F  T  K  Y  R  T  L  U  O  P
J  R  S  K  T  N  A  E  J  P  V  V  O  E  B
T  F  R  T  Y  S  C  N  Z  C  Z  V  K  C  Z
J  U  C  O  I  S  Q  S  Y  B  E  W  O  N  K
T  T  J  P  Q  C  T  J  R  U  J  R  V  O  C
T  I  N  F  M  Z  I  N  Q  L  N  B  Z  M  B
L  J  A  S  V  H  C  D  D  L  S  W  O  C  U
Z  P  Y  L  S  J  B  H  E  S  A  H  Z  T  H
W  N  M  J  X  Q  P  V  K  S  R  F  B  U  Q
I  U  I  W  Z  Y  A  A  K  M  F  A  S  X  E
```

BULLS

CATTLE

CHICKENS

CORN

COWS

CROPS

FARMER

PESTICIDES

POULTRY

TRACTOR

TURKEY

WHEAT

Adverbs of Manner; Adjectives and Adverbs of Manner with the Same Form

PART ONE	Adverbs of Manner

A Complete the sentences with the adverb form of the adjective in parentheses. Then draw an arrow to the verb the adverb is modifying.

1. She spoke ← _nervously_ (nervous) to the police officer.

2. The children always walk _____ (happy) to the park.

3. I don't know her very _____ (good).

4. Volunteers _____ (brave) fight forest fires every year in California.

5. She spoke to the children _____ (firm).

6. My family eats very _____ (healthy).

7. The toddler hung on to her mother _____ (tight).

8. I wake up _____ (easy) every morning at 6:00 AM.

9. Taxi drivers drive _____ (dangerous) in Istanbul.

10. She spoke _____ (worried) to the policeman about her son.

11. He cooks very _____ (simple).

12. They write to each other _____ (secret).

B Read the sentences with adjectives. Write a similar sentence with an adverb.

1. He's a quick worker. _____ He works quickly. _____

2. She's a slow eater. _____

3. They're loud talkers. _____

4. I'm a healthy eater. _____

5. He's a dangerous driver. _____

6. She's a patient listener. _____

C Complete the sentence with an adjective or an adverb.

1. (slow) She spoke _____*slowly*_____ to the foreigner.

2. (nervous) They looked _____ on stage.

3. (good) I didn't look _____ at the prom. My dress was too big.

4. (sad) It was a _____ movie.

5. (firm) My brother has a _____ handshake.

6. (gentle) He spoke _____ to the children.

D Make a sentence with the words given.

1. spoke / her / friend / to / she / secretly

_____ *She spoke to her friend secretly.* _____

2. to / nervously / sing / they / began

_____

3. my / makes / brother / easily / friends

_____

4. bravely / they / walked / into / storm / the

_____

5. always / quietly / teachers / the / in the classroom / talk

_____

6. the / talk / happily / children / their projects / about

_____

7. was / acting / the / patient / dangerously

_____

8. getting / better / was / he / slowly

_____

A Read the sentences. Decide if the underlined word is an adverb or an adjective.

1. Making decisions is <u>hard</u>.   _____*adj.*_____

2. He drives a <u>fast</u> car.   _____

3. She does yoga <u>wrong</u>.   _____

4. She doesn't breathe <u>right</u>.   _____

5. It's raining <u>hard</u>.   _____

6. Lucy's husband is out of the hospital; he's <u>well</u> again.   _____

7. I don't speak English very <u>well</u>.   _____

8. We took a <u>wrong</u> turn yesterday and got lost.   _____

9. She doesn't do the <u>right</u> breathing.   _____

10. She's coming <u>right</u> now.   _____

11. I walk <u>fast</u>.   _____

12. She fell down <u>hard</u>.   _____

 ## Putting It Together

■ GRAMMAR

A Circle the correct adjective or adverb.

Cesar: Hi, Marina. How are you doing?

Marina: I'm doing (well)/ good. How about you?

Cesar: I'm <u>right / all right</u>.

Marina: Are you going to therapy?

Cesar: Yes. But it's <u>hardly / hard</u>.

Marina: I know. But you're taking the <u>right / wrong</u> steps.

Cesar: I know I'm not going to recover <u>quickly / quick</u>.

Marina: Your therapist is very <u>well / good</u>. He treated me
         <u>successfully / successful</u>!

Cesar: Did you recover <u>fast / quick</u>?

Marina:　No. The recovery was <u>slowly / slow</u>. Two years. But I'm eating <u>healthy / healthily</u> now.

Cesar:　You look <u>great / greatly</u>!

Marina:　Thanks.

B **Rewrite the sentences that have mistakes. If there are no mistakes, write "C."**

1. The doctor told firmly her that she had to get treatment. _The doctor told her firmly that she had to get treatment._

2. The baker decorated the cake simply. _____

3. She quickly ran the race. _____

4. They were sitting quiet in the kitchen. _____

5. I hope your teacher is friend. _____

6. It's hard to eat good. _____

7. They sang the songs wrongly. _____

8. She lost dangerously weight. _____

Use the clues to solve the puzzle.

Across

6. treats a patient

7. uses the services of a professional

Down

1. pills or liquid you take as medical treatment

2. to throw up food

3. treatment of a condition or disease

4. improve

5. not be well

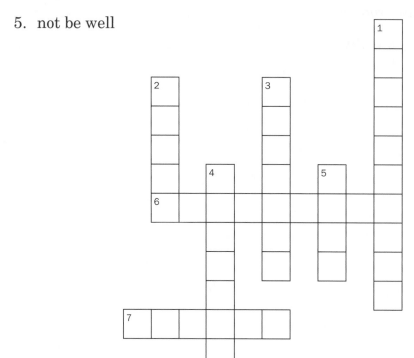

Lesson 15

As...As; The Same as, Similar to, Different from

PART ONE   *As...As*

A Complete the sentences.

1. Riding the train to work is (quick) ___*as quick as*___ driving your car.

2. Using a dictionary is not (easy) _____ using the computer to find a word.

3. Writing an instant message is not (fast) _____ talking on the phone.

4. Helicopters don't fly (high) _____ airplanes.

5. I don't cook (good) _____ my mother.

6. My sister talks (loud) _____ I do.

B Write sentences that have the same meaning. (Answers may vary.)

1. I can run a 7-minute mile.   Kim can run an 8-minute mile.

   _____*Kim can't run as fast as I can.*_____

2. Helen is 5 feet 6 inches.   I'm 5 feet 6 inches.

   _____

3. The chocolate cake tastes good.   The carrot cake tastes good, too.

   _____

4. We have five people in our family.   They have eight people in their family.

   _____

5. Hector is 25 years old.   Olivia is 16 years old.

   _____

6. Daniel has 10 dollars in his wallet.   James has 15 dollars in his wallet.

   _____

C Complete the sentences with *as...as* and the adverbs in parentheses.

1. I work fast. I can write a business plan in (little) ___as little as___ one week.

2. These books are on sale. You can buy (many) _____ you want.

3. Recipe #1 uses 1 cup of sugar. Recipe #2 doesn't use (much) _____ Recipe #1.

4. Rizoni Online University is great. You can complete a degree in (few) _____ 20 months.

5. There are a lot of choices for mobile phone plans. You can get a plan for (little) _____ $20.00 a month.

D Read the information. Write a descriptive sentence using *nearly, almost,* and *about*. Use each adverb once.

1. House A: 1200 square feet   House B: 1250 square feet

   _____House A is nearly as big as House B._____

2. Denver, Colorado, is 5,430 feet above sea level. Colorado Springs, Colorado, is 6,035 feet above sea level.

   _____

3. A gallon of milk costs $3.09. A gallon of regular gasoline costs $3.00.

   _____

4. My house was built in 1910. My friend's house was built in 1899.

   _____

PART TWO	*The Same as, Similar to, Different from*

A Read the information and complete the sentences with *the same as, similar to,* or *different from*.

1. Computer A: $1,750   Computer B: $1,800
   The cost of Computer A is ___similar to___ the cost of Computer B.

2. Conversation 101: 90 minutes   Grammar 103: 50 minutes
   The class time for Conversation 101 is _____ the class time for Grammar 103.

3. House A: 1200 square meters   House B: 1200 square meters.

   The size of House A is _____ the size of House B.

4. Flight to Houston from New York: $230   Flight to Tampa from New York: $219

   The cost of the flight from New York to Houston is _____ the
   cost from New York to Tampa.

5. Angela makes $52,000 a year.   Mohammed makes $68,000.

   Angela's salary is _____ Mohammed's salary.

6. Trip to Alaska: 5 days—$2,500   Trip to Hawaii: 6 days—$2,300

   The trip to Alaska is _____ the trip to Hawaii.

B Write two observations about the information. Use *the same*, *similar to*, and *different from* and the word or phrases in parentheses.

1. Rachel's Dog: German Shepard   Joe's Dog: Chihuahua
   (their dogs) _Their dogs are different._
   (Rachel's dog) _Rachel's dog is different from Joe's dog._

2. Sandra: 120 lbs   Karenina: 120 lbs
   (their weight) _____
   (Sandra weighs) _____

3. My house: 3 bedrooms, 2 baths   Juan's house: 4 bedrooms, 2.5 baths
   (our houses) _____
   (my house) _____

4. Clara's car: four door sedan   Ali's car: SUV
   (their cars) _____
   (Clara's car) _____

5. Her computer: iMac®   His computer: PC
   (their computers) _____
   (her computer) _____

6. Sebastian's hair color: brown   Violet's hair color: brown
   (their hair color) _____
   (Sebastian's hair color) _____

Putting It Together

■ GRAMMAR

A Underline all the grammar points from Lesson 15: *as...as, the same as, similar to, different from, nearly, almost, about.*

Sam: Carla, what's it like in Lima? Is Lima <u>similar to</u> Tucson?

Carla: No. Lima and Tucson are really different. Tucson isn't as big as Lima. Tucson has less than 1 million people; Lima has almost 8 million people.

Sam: Wow! Is the climate in Lima similar to the climate in Tucson?

Carla: No. Lima isn't as hot as Tucson.

Sam: But Lima is in South America!

Carla: Yes, but it's on the coast and it gets a lot of wind from the South Pole. It's cool. It's not as sunny as Tucson. Although it doesn't rain a lot, there are a lot of clouds.

Sam: What about rain? It rains as little as 10 inches a year here in Tucson.

Carla: The rainfall in Lima is similar to the rainfall in Tucson. Lima receives about 6 inches a year. But it's more humid in Lima than in Tucson.

Sam: What about altitude? Tucson is a little high. It's nearly 2,500 feet above sea level.

Carla: The altitude in Lima is different from the altitude in Tucson. Lima is lower than Tucson. It's only about 60 feet above sea level.

Sam: Tucson is definitely not the same as Lima.

Carla: But I still love it. It's my home now!

B Complete the chart with information from the conversation. (Answers may vary.)

	Lima	Tucson	Comparative Phrase
population	almost 8 million	less than 1 million	different
climate			
rain			
humidity			
altitude			

Find the words in the puzzle below and circle them.

```
F  H  E  X  S  R  F  P  M  S  F  Y  F  B  K
O  L  Y  L  K  E  E  O  M  R  J  S  E  W  E
I  W  A  I  T  T  E  U  G  E  V  A  O  C  K
B  N  L  S  B  E  T  N  Z  T  K  T  H  W  I
P  O  C  J  K  M  Y  D  Q  E  L  R  S  O  S
F  N  L  H  T  M  N  S  R  M  E  R  N  E  R
X  L  Q  T  E  N  G  A  M  I  E  Q  L  B  Y
S  C  A  L  E  S  R  E  W  T  S  I  C  D  Q
Q  S  H  E  G  N  E  Z  E  N  M  T  L  D  Y
H  S  X  E  K  H  Z  M  A  E  R  V  K  T  L
N  T  O  O  X  P  O  A  L  C  N  E  D  U  J
M  I  I  X  U  L  T  C  R  N  X  A  L  B  F
O  Z  J  M  I  C  R  O  S  C  O  P  E  U  U
P  W  C  K  N  T  P  P  G  A  N  V  Z  A  R
C  J  O  T  V  N  O  T  Y  U  J  H  W  P  R
```

BEAKER

CENTIMETERS

FEET

FLASK

INCHES

KILO

KILOMETERS

MAGNET

METER

MICROSCOPE

MILES

POUNDS

RULER

SCALE

TON

The Simple Past Tense: Statements with Regular Verbs; The Simple Past Tense: Yes/No Questions and Short Answers

PART ONE	**The Simple Past Tense: Statements with Regular Verbs**

A Write the verbs in the past tense.

1. study ___studied___
2. help _____
3. protest _____
4. lift _____
5. offer _____

6. celebrate _____
7. work _____
8. travel _____
9. ship _____
10. press _____

11. smile _____
12. import _____
13. touch _____
14. produce _____
15. vote _____

B Write the verbs from exercise A in the pronunciation chart below.

/d/	/t/	/id/
studied		

C Complete the sentences with the verbs in parentheses. The first sentence is affirmative. The second sentence is negative. Use contractions.

1. (study)   I ___studied___ Spanish in high school.

   I ___didn't study___ it in college.

2. (work)   They _____ at the office until 9:00 last night.

   They _____ tonight.

3. (import)   My father's company _____ products from China.

   They _____ anything from India.

4. (offer)   The president of the company _____ me a part-time job.

He _____ me a full-time job.

5. (ship)   They _____ the products by boat.

               They _____ them by plane.

6. (travel)   He _____ to Antarctica last year.

               He _____ to the Arctic.

7. (vote)   We _____ in the state election.

               We _____ in the national election.

8. (celebrate) They _____ their wedding anniversary on the 10th.

               They _____ it on the 11th.

PART TWO	The Simple Past Tense: *Yes/No* Questions and Short Answers

A Write *yes/no* questions for the answers. Then complete the short answers.

1. _____ Did your parents immigrate to the United States from Ecuador? _____

   Yes, my parents immigrated to
   the United States from Ecuador.   Yes, _they did._

2. _____

   No, they didn't travel by airplane.   No, _____

3. _____

   Yes, my aunt joined them.   Yes, _____

4. _____

   Yes, my grandparents stayed in Ecuador. Yes, _____

5. _____

   Yes, I arrived with my family.   Yes, _____

6. _____

   No, we didn't live in California first. No, _____

7. _____

   Yes, my family received help from
   an organization.   Yes, _____

8. _____

   Yes, my father looked for a job right away. Yes, _____

9. _____

   No, we didn't stay in California very long. No, _____

B Write a question in the past tense with the words in parentheses. Then provide a true short answer.

1. (help / your friend / today)

   _____ Did you help your friend today? _____

   _____ Yes, I did. OR No, I didn't. _____

2. (celebrate / your birthday / last week)

   _____

   _____

3. (work / today)

   _____

   _____

4. (smile / at your teacher)

   _____

   _____

5. (lift / anything heavy)

   _____

   _____

6. (travel / anywhere by car / today)

   _____

   _____

7. (touch / an animal / today)

   _____

   _____

8. (offer / money to anyone / today)

   _____

   _____

Putting It Together

■ **GRAMMAR**

A Complete the dialogue with the correct tense of the verb in parentheses.

Simon: _____ Did _____ your parents _____ arrive _____ (arrive)?

Erica: Yes, _____ they did. _____ They _____ (arrive) last night.

Simon: Were they tired?

Erica: Yes, _____ . They _____ (not sleep) on the plane.

Simon: _____ your aunt _____ (travel) with them?

Erica: No, _____ . She _____ (need) to stay home with her children.

Simon: _____ your parents _____ (stay) at your house or in a hotel?

Erica: They're staying at our house.

Simon: How long _____ they _____ (stay)?

Erica: Six months.

Simon: Wow! That's a long time. What _____ they _____ (do) when you're at work?

Erica: A lot. They _____ (exercise). They _____ (shop). Sometimes they _____ (go) to the beach. My mother _____ (prepare) dinner for us. They _____ (clean) the house. And sometimes my father _____ (pick up) the children from school.

Simon: That's great! They're very helpful.

Erica: Yes. I like having them here.

B **Rewrite the sentences with mistakes. If there are no mistakes, write "C."**

1. He did'nt go to work today.   _He didn't go to work today._

2. He studied at my school last year.   _____

3. We didn't talk to them in the library. _____

4. I didn't wanted to go.   _____

5. My grandparents immigrated to the United States last year. _____

6. We live in Canada first.   _____

7. Did you received the letter?   _____

8. Did she decide to joined the army?   _____

Unscramble each of the clue words. Use the numbered letters to complete the sentence at the bottom.

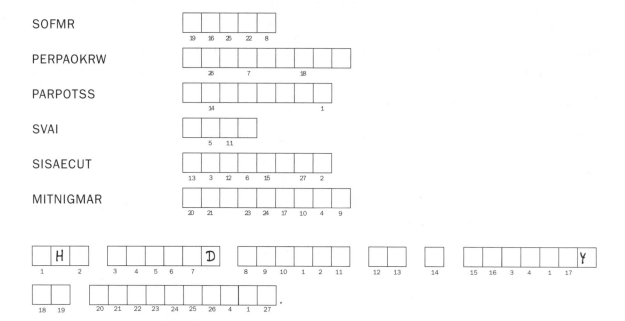

SOFMR

19 16 25 22 8

PERPAOKRW

26   7   18

PARPOTSS

14   1

SVAI

5 11

SISAECUT

13 3 12 6 15   27 2

MITNIGMAR

20 21   23 24 17 10 4 9

H | D | | | | Y

1 2   3 4 5 6 7   8 9 10 1 2 11   12 13   14   15 16 3 4 1 17

18 19   20 21 22 23 24 25 26 4 1 27 .

The Simple Past Tense: Irregular Verbs; The Simple Past Tense: Information Questions; *Before* and *After* in the Simple Past Tense

PART ONE	The Simple Past Tense: Irregular Verbs

A Complete the sentences with the verb in the past tense.

1. The baby _____*drank*_____ (drink) all the milk.

2. I _____ (think) people in Brazil spoke Spanish.

3. We _____ (read) that book in class.

4. She _____ (know) the manager of the restaurant.

5. He _____ (take) a pencil from the table.

6. Madonna _____ (become) famous in 1982.

7. I _____ (cut) my finger on the glass.

8. They _____ (come) home late last night.

9. We _____ (eat) a lot during Thanksgiving last year.

10. He _____ (give) his mother flowers for Mother's Day.

11. I _____ (break) my leg when I was ten.

12. The man _____ (find) $100 on the sidewalk.

13. The child _____ (begin) preschool last week.

14. She _____ (do) her homework in an hour.

15. We _____ (be) in the same English class last year.

16. The elderly woman _____ (fight) the mugger in the street.

17. I _____ (keep) the pictures of my high school boyfriend.

18. You _____ (write) me only one e-mail this week.

19. They all _____ (have) the flu last winter.

20. I _____ (feel) sick after dinner tonight.

B Use the phrases in parentheses to write a sentence in the negative.

1. (find $100 in the street)

   I didn't find $100 in the street.

2. (read the newspaper this morning)

   _____

3. (drink too much coffee)

   _____

4. (feel well this morning)

   _____

5. (do my homework)

   _____

6. (give my friend a ride to class today)

   _____

7. (eat lunch today)

   _____

8. (take the bus to class)

   _____

C Write a *yes/no* question from the phrases below. Then respond to the question with a true short answer.

1. (come to class early)

   Did you come to class early?   _Yes, I did._ OR _No, I didn't._

2. (have breakfast this morning)

   _____   _____

3. (walk to class from home)

   _____   _____

4. (feel well yesterday)

   _____   _____

5. (break a glass today)

   _____   _____

6. (have a good day)

   _____   _____

7. (do your laundry last night)

   _____   _____

8. (think that English was easy)

   _____   _____

A Write *wh-* questions for the answers. Use *when, where, how, who,* and *what.*

1. _____ *When did you go home yesterday?* _____

   I went home <u>at 3:30</u>.

2. _____

   They lived <u>in Minnesota</u> first.

3. _____

   She did <u>well</u> on the test.

4. _____

   <u>My mother</u> made the cake.

5. _____

   We <u>went to the movies</u> last night.

6. _____

   I found <u>a puppy</u> yesterday.

7. _____

   <u>My parents</u> gave me the car.

8. _____

   She broke it <u>yesterday</u>.

9. _____

   We went <u>to the Bahamas</u> for vacation.

10. _____

I felt <u>terrible</u> during the test.

11. _____

I read <u>a magazine</u> on the train.

12. _____

<u>My friend</u> called.

A **Match the time clause with the most appropriate action.**

1. After I exercised at the gym, __j__   a. we set the table.

2. After we had dinner, _____   b. I worked for a year.

3. Before we ate dinner, _____   c. he read a chapter in the book.

4. After she plugged in the computer, _____   d. I turned off the light.

5. Before I went to college, _____   e. they got out of the car.

6. Before he fell asleep, _____   f. we washed the dishes.

7. After I left the room, _____   g. she took the baby's temperature.

8. After they parked, _____   h. she turned it on.

9. Before she called the doctor, _____   i. I gave it to my instructor.

10. After I finished my homework, _____   j. I took a shower.

B **Write a time clause to complete each sentence. Write four sentences with *after* and four with *before*.**

    After I did my homework, I watched TV.

1. _____ I ate breakfast.

2. _____ I left the house.

3. _____ I opened the door.

4. _____ I called my family.

5. _____ I read the newspaper.

6. _____ I cleaned the house.

7. _____ I set the alarm clock.

8. _____ I washed my hands.

Putting It Together

■ GRAMMAR

A Complete the dialogue with the questions from the box. Then complete the answers with the past tense of the verb in parentheses.

How did you get there?	Did you like the concert?
Did you do anything after the concert?	Who went to the concert?
Did you do anything else?	What did you do last night?
Where did you eat?	Why did you go straight home?
Who did you see?	

Alan: _____ *What did you do last night?* _____

Tatiana: We _____ (go) to a rock concert.

Alan: _____

Tatiana: My brother Sam and our cousins, Felipe and Alexandra.

Alan: _____

Tatiana: Sam _____ (drive) us.

Alan: _____

Tatiana: Yes! It was great.

Alan: _____

Tatiana: We _____ (see) Black Angel.

Alan: I _____ (think) that they broke up.

Tatiana: No, they didn't.

Alan: _____

Tatiana: Before the concert, we _____ (have) dinner.

Alan: _____

Tatiana: We _____ (eat) at Pepe's Pizza.

Alan: _____

Tatiana: No. After the concert, we _____ (go) straight home.

Alan: _____

Tatiana: We were really tired.

B **Rewrite the sentences with mistakes. If there are no mistakes, write "C."**

1. She drinked the tea.   _____She drank the tea._____

2. I didn't wrote to you.   _____

3. Why did you immigrate to
   the United States?   _____

4. How long ago you come here?   _____

5. Who got married in church yesterday?   _____

6. Before we move to Nevada, we
   lived in Utah.   _____

7. What you did yesterday?   _____

8. He break the plate at dinner.   _____

9. Did you cut your finger?   _____

10. Where did you went last night?   _____

11. They became famous overnight.   _____

12. Who did arrive to class late?   _____

Use the clues to solve the puzzle.

Across

4.   organ that controls thought

5.   treatment of injuries by incision

6.   organ that cleans blood

8.   medical doctor who performs operations or surgeries

Down

1.   breathing organs

2.   pumps blood through the body

3.   carry blood from the heart

4.   red liquid in the body

7.   carry blood to the heart

The Past Progressive: Statements;
The Past Progressive: Questions

PART ONE   The Past Progressive: Statements

A Complete the sentences in the affirmative with the verb in the past progressive.

1. She ___*was watching*___ (watch) TV all afternoon.

2. The Garcias _____ (talk) with their neighbors during the barbeque.

3. My brother _____ (help) my mother at the party.

4. I _____ (wait) for the bus at 3:00.

5. We _____ (visit) our grandparents last month.

6. The instructors _____ (have) a meeting in the other room.

7. Last year the company _____ (import) products from China.

8. Yesterday we _____ (sell) a lot of books.

9. The price of gas _____ (fall) last week.

10. Loggers _____ (pollute) rivers in the Amazon.

11. The fax machine _____ (work) yesterday.

12. The doctor _____ (operate) on the young patient.

B Rewrite the sentences in the negative. Use the words in parentheses to write a sentence in the positive that corrects the first. Use contractions appropriately.

1. At 11:00 my son was sleeping. (read)

   _____*At 11:00 my son wasn't sleeping. He was reading.*_____

2. Yesterday my friends were having a meeting. (a party)

   _____

3. In the movie the lions were swimming. (hunt)

   _____

4. The children were crying. (play)

_____

5. They were dancing in the cafeteria. (eating)

_____

6. It was raining all morning. (snow)

_____

C **What were you doing at these times yesterday? Write a sentence for each time.**

Time	Activity
6:00 AM	
8:00 AM	
10:00 AM	
12:00 PM	
2:00 PM	
4:00 PM	
6:00 PM	
8:00 PM	
10:00 PM	
12:00 AM	

PART TWO **The Past Progressive: Questions**

A **Write questions with the words in parentheses. Use the past progressive. Then complete the short answers.**

1. (you / make a phone call)   _Were you making a phone call?_

   Yes, _____ _I was._ _____

2. (she / look for her wallet)   _____

   No, _____

3. (the radio / play our song)   _____

   Yes, _____

4. (the dog / dig in the garden)   _____

   No, _____

5. (children / hide)   _____

Yes, _____

6. (we / go to class)   _____

No, _____

B Write an information question for the answer.

1. _____ *What were you doing yesterday?* _____

I was <u>researching dinosaurs</u> in the library yesterday.

2. _____

Frank was studying <u>archaeology</u> last semester.

3. _____

We were listening to music <u>at Cesar's house</u>.

4. _____

We went to Cesar's house <u>because he has a new stereo</u>.

5. _____

They were working <u>at 6:00</u>.

6. _____

I was watching TV for <u>two hours</u>.

7. _____

She was calling <u>her parents</u>.

8. _____

He was looking for <u>his wallet</u>.

9. _____

He was looking for his wallet <u>because he lost it yesterday</u>.

■ GRAMMAR

A Complete the questions with missing words.

1. Alex: _____*Where*_____ were you going last night?
    Pablo: I was walking to class.

2. James: _____ you _____ for your cell phone?
    Rula: No, I wasn't. I was looking for my money.

3. Matt: _____ were you eating at breakfast?
    Marlene: We were eating salmon and noodles.

4. Puja: _____ was studying in Seattle last year?
    Laura: My sister was.

5. Eva: _____ were you living in England?
    Gustavo: Six years.

6. Lin: _____ are you walking to class?
    Tom: My car is broken.

B Complete the short answers.

1. Sandra: Were you expecting to get an A in Mr. Albert's class?
    Marco: Yes, _____*I was.*_____

2. Raul: Was he talking about dinosaurs again?
    Rula: No, _____

3. Fedor: Weren't you watching TV last night?
    Liz: No, _____

4. Nina: Was she planning to study English in the United States?
    Laura: Yes, _____

5. Zoe: Were they protecting the trees in the forest?
    Maya: No, _____

C Choose the best response for each question.

1. What was she doing in the shopping center?
   (a.) She was buying a   b. She went in.   c. She sat down.
       computer.

2. Were you watching TV?
   a. No, I didn't.   b. No, I wasn't.   c. No, I didn't watch.

3. Who were you looking for?
   a. The instructor was   b. I was.   c. For the instructor.
      looking for me.

4. Were they studying paleontology?
   a. I was studying   b. Yes, he was.   c. No, they weren't.
      physics.

5. Why was he calling his instructor?
   a. He can't go to class   b. He's a student.   c. He's the instructor.
      tomorrow.

6. Where were you going last night?
   a. To the movies.   b. No, we weren't.   c. Yes, we were.

7. How long were you doing your homework?
   a. I was not.   b. I wasn't   c. Two hours.

8. Were they driving all day?
   a. Yes, they were.   b. Yes, they drove.   c. Yes, they did.

9. What was happening in class this morning when you got there?
   a. The students took   b. The teacher was   c. The students
      a test.   late.   were taking a test.

10. Who were you talking to?
    a. I was talking to the   b. He was talking.   c. Yes, I was.
       operator.   to me.

■ VOCABULARY

Unscramble the tiles to reveal a message.

AND		HU	TIN	NG		SAU	INO	ERE	NTI

MAL	G	D	MAM		EA	RS.		S	W

When with the Simple Past Tense and Past Progressive; *While* with the Simple Past Tense and Past Progressive

PART ONE

***When* with the Simple Past Tense and Past Progressive**

A Combine phrases in Column A and Column B to make sentences with *when* in the simple past. Use each phrase once.

A	B
~~the storm struck~~	I hung up the telephone
my mother received the news	the musicians got quiet
the strange man called	the citizens rioted in the streets
he opened the door	~~our basement flooded~~
the conductor raised her baton	the students put away their notes
the band started playing	she fainted
she became president	they closed the door
they got into the room	he listened to his voicemail
the instructor passed out the exam	I walked in
he turned on his telephone	I couldn't hear anything

1. When the storm struck, our basement flooded.
2.
3.
4.
5.
6.
7.
8.
9.
10.

B Complete the sentences with the correct form of the verb.

1. I ___was talking___ (talk) on the phone when my friends
   ___walked in___ (walk in).

2. We _____ (eat) dinner when the telemarketer
   _____ (call).

3. When the comic _____ (perform), the waitress
   _____ (drop) the tray.

4. They _____ (walk) down the street when the tree
   _____ (fall).

5. We _____ (look) for the little boy when the police
   _____ (arrive).

6. When we _____ (run), Angela _____ (fall).

7. When we _____ (pass) the truck, someone _____
   (beep) their horn.

8. I _____ (listen to) my iPod® when the batteries
   _____ (die).

9. She _____ (walk) the dog when a car _____ (hit) her.

10. The airplane _____ (land) when the pilot _____
    (make) the announcement.

PART TWO   *While* with the Simple Past Tense and Past Progressive

---

A Complete the sentences with the correct form of the verb.

1. While I ___was working___ (work) on the computer, my brother
   ___walked___ (walk) in.

2. While I _____ (listen) to the radio, I _____ (fall)
   asleep.

3. My father _____ (start) to fall asleep while he
   _____ (drive).

4. While she _____ (walk) out the door, she _____
   (hear) someone call her name.

5. We _____ (learn) a lot about different cultures while we
   _____ (travel) in Asia.

6. A snake _____ (bite) me while I _____ (walk) through the tall grass.

7. While they _____ (stand) outside, it _____ (start) to rain.

8. The alarm clock _____ (ring) twice while I _____ (sleep).

B Write a sentence with *while* and the simple past tense and past progressive using the words in parentheses.

1. (read) _____ While I was reading, the doorbell rang. _____

2. (study) _____

3. (watch TV) _____

4. (go to class) _____

5. (have dinner) _____

6. (exercise) _____

7. (read the newspaper) _____

8. (cross the street) _____

9. (sleep) _____

10. (talk to a friend) _____

Putting It Together

■ GRAMMAR

A Fill in the blanks with *while* or *when*. In some cases, both *when* and *while* can be used.

1. _____ When _____ I renovated my house, I installed new locks.

2. The police stopped us _____ we were trying to cross the street.

3. The DVD got stuck _____ I was watching the movie.

4. _____ the movie ended, we walked home.

5. _____ we were taking a break, the teacher showed us some pictures.

6. We went out to dinner _____ we left the office.

7. The little boy opened the door _____ the car was moving.

8. _____ the plane was in the air, the engine stalled.

B **Rewrite the sentences correctly.**

1. I'm walking down the street when I saw the car accident.

    I was walking down the street when I saw the car accident.

2. The archaeologist was digging when he finds the mummy.

    _____

3. While they ate, the music played.

    _____

4. We were playing soccer when the lightning was striking.

    _____

5. When the lights were turning off, she left the room.

    _____

6. When the rain stopped, the children were going out to play.

    _____

7. The monkeys were playing in the trees when we walk through the jungle.

    _____

8. I woke up when the sun rises.

    _____

■ VOCABULARY

Unscramble each of the clue words. Use the numbered letters to complete the sentence at the bottom.

RENGILIO

	2		6		12		11

MEEPTL

9	21	26	16		13

RPTESI

24		27	5	7	17

NYGRIAP

4	23	15	10	20	14

PECHES

22		3	19		18

WODCR

25		1	28

							V																					
1	2		1	3	4	5		6	7	8	9	10	11	12		13	14	15	16	17		1	18	19	20		1	21

22	23	1		9	18	3		24	15	25	23	26	27	28	7

Should, Ought To, Must Not; Have To, Must, Had To

PART ONE	*Should, Ought To, Must Not*

A Make suggestions using *should* and *ought to*.

1. I'm thirsty.

   You _____ *ought to drink something.* _____

2. I don't feel well.

   You _____

3. My father is 65 years old. He still works everyday.

   He _____

4. Anna's birthday is next week.

   We _____

5. We're going to be late for class.

   We _____

6. I'm bored.

   You _____

7. I watch five hours of TV a day.

   You _____

8. Erica wants to buy a car.

   She _____

9. My friends stay up late every night. They're always tired in class.

   They _____

10. My eyes hurt when I read.

    You _____

B Circle the correct modal.

1. Twelve-year-olds (shouldn't /(mustn't)) drive a car.

2. You (shouldn't / mustn't) eat too much ice cream. You'll get sick!

3. You (shouldn't / mustn't) drive without a license.

4. You (shouldn't / mustn't) walk your dog without a leash.

5. You (shouldn't / mustn't) ignore traffic signals.

6. You (shouldn't / mustn't) argue with a police officer.

7. You (shouldn't / mustn't) bring knives onto an airplane.

8. You (shouldn't / mustn't) walk alone at night.

9. You (shouldn't / mustn't) park in a handicapped parking space if you don't have a handicapped parking permit.

10. You (shouldn't / mustn't) call 911 as a joke or prank.

11. You (shouldn't / mustn't) buy a brand new car.

12. You (shouldn't / mustn't) waste water.

C Complete the sentences with *should, ought to, shouldn't,* or *mustn't.* Some answers may vary.

1. Gas prices are very high. I _____*ought to*_____ buy a hybrid car.

2. There's a sign by the lake that says *No Swimming*. You _____ go swimming there.

3. You _____ exercise at least three times a week.

4. In social settings you _____ introduce women first.

5. When you are introduced to an American, you _____ shake his hand firmly.

6. You _____ eat with your mouth full.

7. When you're eating, you _____ put your elbows on the table.

8. You _____ fix your hair in public.

9. You _____ use a toothpick at the table.

10. In the state of Connecticut, you _____ smoke inside a public building.

11. You _____ tip your waiter 15–20%.

12. You _____ talk loud on your cell phone in public.

13. You _____ leave a child under the age of 12 unattended in a car.

14. Drivers in New Jersey _____ use their cell phones while driving.

A **Write five sentences with *have to* and five sentences with *must*. Use the phrases in the chart below. Write the sentences in any order.**

I have to	You must
~~call my grandmother~~	~~walk your dog on a leash~~
exercise more	get a new driver's license
eat less fatty food	wear glasses driving if you need them
learn another language	prepare taxes before April 15th
learn English	renew your visa next month

1. _____ I have to call my grandmother. _____

2. _____ You must walk your dog on a leash. _____

3. _____

4. _____

5. _____

6. _____

7. _____

8. _____

9. _____

10. _____

B **Write three things you have to do now, three things you don't have to do now, and three things you must not do in your home country.**

have to do now

1. _____

2. _____

3. _____

don't have to do now

1. _____
2. _____
3. _____

must do in my home country

1. _____
2. _____
3. _____

C Write questions for the answers given.

1. _____ *Do you have to go to basketball practice tonight?* _____

   Yes, I have to go to basketball practice tonight.

2. _____

   No, I don't have to do any homework tonight.

3. _____

   Yes, she had to take a taxi home.

4. _____

   Yes, they must report to work every morning.

5. _____

   No, they didn't have to call the doctor.

6. _____

   Yes, we have to call Jenny now.

7. _____

   Yes, everyone must file a tax return.

Putting It Together

■ **GRAMMAR**

A Complete the conversations by circling the correct words.

1. A: Do you (have to)/ had to go to class today?
   B: No, I don't.

2. A: What are you doing today?
   B: I <u>mustn't / don't have to</u> do anything. I can take the day off.

3. A: Are there any rules in the gym?
   B: Yes. Everyone <u>have to / must</u> take off their shoes before entering the gym. You can only wear sneakers.

4. A: I'm so hungry!
   B: Well. You <u>ought to / shouldn't</u> eat something.

5. A: Why is the boss mad at me?
   B: You <u>don't have to / mustn't</u> sleep at your desk!

6. A: Did you get up early today?
   B: No. I <u>didn't have to / shouldn't</u>. I don't work today.

7. A: Ken <u>ought to / has to</u> give me $20.00.
   B: Why?
   A: I gave him $20.00 last week.

8. A: What <u>should / must</u> I do on my first day of class?
   B: You <u>shouldn't / ought to</u> talk a lot. You should listen.

B **Rewrite the sentences with mistakes. If there are no mistakes, write "C."**

1. I must to go to work early today.   _I must go to work early today._

2. You should take a vacation.   _____

3. You ought to get a visa to visit China.   _____

4. We had to bought a new car.   _____

5. Shouldn't you tip the waiter?   _____

6. You don't have to drink alcohol at work.   _____

7. They ought study Spanish.   _____

8. You mustn't watch that movie. It's boring.   _____

9. We must to call the police.   _____

10. She has to find a new job.   _____

■ **V O C A B U L A R Y**

Unscramble the tiles to reveal a message.

| O U L | N T R | L F . | D | I | S H | C E | O D U | R S E |
| Y O U | Y O U |

| | | | | | | |
| | |

I. Topic, Supporting, and Concluding Sentences

A Read the information below.

About Mario

❶Mario is a very busy student. ❷He studies computer science at State University and he also studies English. ❸During the day, he goes to classes. ❹At night, he works in the bookstore. ❺On the weekends, he volunteers at the children's library. ❻Mario doesn't rest!

Sentence ❶ is a **topic sentence.** It covers all of the information in a paragraph. Sentences ❷ ❸ ❹ ❺ are **supporting sentences.** They give facts and descriptions to show that the main point of a paragraph is true. Supporting sentences are clearly connected to the topic sentence. Sentence ❻ is a **concluding sentence.** This sentence summarizes the paragraph.

B Read the paragraph below. Write the topic sentence, four supporting sentences, and the concluding sentence.

The Irish Potato Famine

The Irish Potato Famine **happened** between 1845 and 1849. A disease **destroyed** the potatoes in Ireland. Potatoes were the main food for people in Ireland. People **didn't have** enough food to eat. Almost one million people **died** in the famine. Many Irish **didn't want** to live in Ireland anymore. Nearly 2 million people **immigrated** to the United States. They **traveled** to the United States by ship and **landed** in the big cities of Boston, New York, and Philadelphia. Most of the Irish families **stayed** in these cities. The 1850 census in Boston **showed** that more than 25% of the city was made up of Irish immigrants. The Irish Potato Famine had a major impact on Ireland and the United States.

---

1. Topic sentence: _____

2. Supporting sentences:

    a. (Fact 1) _____

    b. (Fact 2) _____

    c. (Description 1) _____

    d. (Description 2) _____

3. Concluding sentence: _____

II. Writing a Paragraph

C Take notes in the chart about an event that happened in the past.

Event	(Example: The Irish Potato Famine)
Details	(Example: Happened between 1845 and 1849)

D Write a topic sentence and a concluding sentence for your event.

1. Topic sentence: _____

2. Concluding sentence: _____

E Write a paragraph about your event.

F Check your paragraph. Use the checklist.

	Yes	No
Good paragraph form (see p. 51)		
Good punctuation (see p. 51)		
Topic sentence		
Supporting sentences		
Concluding sentence		
Grammar from lessons 11–20		

G Rewrite your paragraph.

Can, May for Permssion; Can, Could, Would for Requests; Want, Would Like for Desires

PART ONE	Can, May for Permssion; Can, Could, Would for Requests

A Ask permission using the words in parentheses.

1. (can / come in) _____ Can I come in? _____

2. (could / call you) _____

3. (may / use the bathroom) _____

4. (could / I take a brochure) _____

5. (can / use your phone) _____

6. (may / have a drink of water) _____

7. (could / see your photos) _____

8. (can / come over now) _____

B Make a request using the words in parentheses.

1. (can / help me) _____ Can you help me? _____

2. (could / lend me money) _____

3. (would / close the door) _____

4. (would / make dinner) _____

5. (can / make a reservation) _____

6. (could / be quiet) _____

7. (would / give me a lift) _____

C Decide if the speaker is asking permission or making a request.

	Permission	Request
1. May I borrow your pen?	✔	
2. Can you fix the sink?		
3. Could you call John?		
4. Can I walk with you?		
5. Could I have a bite?		
6. Can you repeat what you said?		
7. Would you check out, please?		
8. May I speak with the desk clerk?		
9. Would you turn off the lights?		
10. Could I see the guest book?		

D Write negative responses.

1. May I go to the party?

    No, you may not go to the party.

2. Can I call my friends?

3. May I have more cake?

4. Can we go to the movies?

5. Can Isabel stay over tonight?

6. May we play outside?

7. Can you help the customers?

8. Can you buy me a new bike?

9. Can Pablo eat dinner with us?

10. May I go on the school trip?

A **Write sentences that express desire.**

1. (would like / a sandwich) _____ Mei would like a sandwich. _____

2. (want / to go home) _____

3. (would like / a room with a view) _____

4. (want / to sleep) _____

5. (would like / fixed rate) _____

6. (want / to talk with you) _____

B **Write yes/no questions for the answers given.**

1. _____ Would you like some iced tea? _____

   Yes, I would like iced tea.

2. _____

   No, I don't want a ride.

3. _____

   Yes, she would like some advice.

4. _____

   No, they don't want a rental car reservation.

5. _____

   Yes, we would like to have a nonsmoking room.

6. _____

   No, he doesn't want to watch TV.

7. _____

   Yes, I would like to make a complaint.

8. _____

   No, I don't want to go to the mall today.

C Write *wh-* questions for the answers given.

1. _____ What would you like to drink? _____

    I'd like <u>lemonade</u>.

2. _____

    I want to go <u>home</u>.

3. _____

    I'd like to speak to <u>the manager</u>.

4. _____

    We would like to borrow <u>$25,000</u>.

5. _____

    They want to go <u>today</u>.

6. _____

    He'd like a <u>nonsmoking</u> room.

7. _____

    We want to <u>take a trip to Mexico</u>.

8. _____

    We'd like to stay <u>two weeks</u>.

Putting It Together

GRAMMAR

A Choose the correct answer.

1. _____ lend me some money?

    a. Can you   b. Can I   c. May you

2. Would your parents like to go to the museum today?

    a. Yes, they do.   b. No, they wouldn't like.   c. Yes, they would.

3. Would you help me clean the kitchen?

    a. Yes, of course.   b. No, I could.   c. Yes, I help

4. Do they want to learn German?

    a. No, they wouldn't.   b. No, they don't.   c. No, they can't.

5. _____ you give me a room with a view?

    a. May   b. Could   c. Would like

6. May we stay out until midnight?

    a. No, you could not.   b. Yes, you may.   c. No, sorry. I'm too busy.

7. Could you give me your telephone number?

    a. Yes, I could.   b. Yes, I may.   c. Yes, I couldn't.

8. Do you want to go out with me tonight?

    a. No, I don't want.   b. Yes, I do.   c. Yes, I want.

9. I _____ to make a reservation.

    a. can   b. could   c. would like

10. Would your friend like to go to the movies tonight?

    a. Yes, he do.   b. No, he wouldn't like.   c. Yes, he would.

11. Can I have a dog?

    a. No, you can.   b. Yes, you can't.   c. No, you cannot.

12. Do you want to pick up the rental car at the airport?

    a. Yes, I would.   b. Yes, I do.   c. No, I couldn't.

B **Rewrite the sentences with mistakes. If there are no mistakes, write "C."**

1. Can you borrow me money?   _Can you lend me money?_

2. Would you like some coffee?   _____

3. May you help me?   _____

4. We'd like check in.   _____

5. I want to go to Cancun this year.   _____

6. Could you come over to my house?   _____

7. Do you help me move this table?   _____

8. Could you spell your name, please.   _____

9. May Marco come to the movies?   _____

10. You want tea?   _____

Unscramble each of the clue words. Use the numbered letters to complete the sentence at the bottom.

SUGTE ▢▢▢▢▢ (11)

DKSE KRLEC ▢▢▢▢ (12) ▢▢▢▢▢ (1)

GIITESNARROT DEKS ▢▢▢▢▢▢▢▢▢▢▢▢ (18)(2)(20) ▢▢▢▢

MEAK A ROSNEVIETAR ▢▢▢▢ ▢ ▢▢▢▢▢▢▢▢▢▢ (9)(3)

KECCH NI ▢▢▢▢▢ ▢▢ (4)

HEKCC TUO ▢▢▢▢▢ (7) ▢▢▢

TEVARL GEATN ▢▢▢▢▢ (14)(6)(15) ▢▢▢▢▢ (16)(13)(17)

SOBREHCUR ▢▢▢▢▢▢▢▢▢ (10)

RUECOMSST ▢▢▢▢▢▢▢▢▢ (19)(5)

CIERUS SIPH ▢▢▢▢▢▢ (8) ▢▢▢▢

▢▢▢ ▢ ▢▢▢▢ ▢ ▢▢▢▢▢▢▢▢▢▢▢ ?
1 2 3 / 4 / 5 6 7 8 / 9 / 10 11 12 13 14 15 16 17 18 19 20

Factual Conditional Statements; Factual Conditional Questions

PART ONE	**Factual Conditional Statements**

A Match the *if/when* clause with the secondary clause.

1. If it looks like it's going to rain, <u>*e*</u>
2. When I buy something, ___
3. If I send a fax, ___
4. When the lake freezes, ___
5. When the dog gets sick, ___
6. When I'm in a meeting, ___
7. When I exercise, ___
8. When I pass people in the hallway, ___
9. When I meet someone new, ___

a. I drink a lot of water.
b. I take a lot of notes.
c. I shake his or her hand firmly.
d. I always send a cover page.
e. I take an umbrella.
f. I smile and greet them.
g. I always keep the receipt.
h. I take him to the vet right away.
i. we go ice skating.

B Write conditional sentences using the words in parentheses and *if.*

1. (want to lose weight / exercise a lot)

    If you want to lose weight, exercise a lot.

2. (need to talk to my brother / call him in the morning)

    _____

3. (have extra time / read a book)

    _____

4. (like to read a lot / join a book club)

    _____

5. (want to search online / type in the keywords)

    _____

6. (download songs online / get the songs you want)

_____

7. (shop online / find better prices)

_____

A Answer the *wh-* questions with the words in parentheses.

1. What do you do if you have a flat tire?

   (change it myself) _____ *If I have a flat tire, I change it myself.* _____

2. What do you do if you want to relax?

   (surf the Web) _____

3. Who does Juan talk to if he has a problem?

   (my sister) _____

4. If you need a vacation, where do you go?

   (to the mountains) _____

5. How do I contact the company if I need to ask a question?

   (send customer service an e-mail) _____

6. If I need an application, where do I go?

   (the administration building) _____

7. Who do they call if I need a ride home?

   (me) _____

8. What do I do if I finish my test early?

   (leave the room) _____

B Write *yes/no* questions for the answers given.

1. _____ *Do I ask you if I have a question about the test?* _____

   Yes, you ask me if you have a question about the test.

2. _____

   No. I don't like to get a massage when I'm stressed out.

3. _____

Absolutely. I like to do yoga if I want to exercise.

4. _____

My parents don't stay with me if they come into town.

5. _____

Yes, we usually get Chinese food if we don't want to cook.

6. _____

No, I don't.

Putting It Together

■ GRAMMAR

A Complete the following sentences with *if* or *when* and any necessary question words. Add commas where necessary.

David: Do you use the Internet __*if*__ you want to call your family?

Cecilia: No, I don't. I use the phone.

David: Is it expensive?

Cecilia: Not really. _____ I want to call _____ I buy a phone card. I can talk for hours for less than five dollars.

David: That's expensive! _____ I want to talk with my family _____ I use the Internet.

Cecilia: _____ you call with the Internet _____ _____ does it cost?

David: Nothing! It's free!

Cecilia: _____ I want to use the Internet _____ _____ do I do?

David: _____ you want to make free calls _____ you need a fast connection. You also need a microphone. Then you download the program from the Internet.

Cecilia: Do I pay anything _____ I download the program?

David: No. The program is free.

Cecilia: Wow! This is great. I'm going to download the program _____ I get home.

Use the clues to solve the puzzle.

Across

4. slow connection

5. what you do with a mouse

7. choose

10. important words

Down

1. address on the Internet

2. what you do with a computer keyboard

3. no wires

6. fast connection

8. connection

9. communication device

The Future with *Be Going To*;
The Future with the Present Progressive

The Future with *Be Going To*

A Write a sentence with *be going to* and the words in parentheses.

1. (I / go to the beach / tomorrow)

   I'm going to go to the beach tomorrow.

2. (he / be a police officer / in two years)

   _____

3. (she / be here / in a few hours)

   _____

4. (we / go to the gym / tonight)

   _____

5. (they / travel to Europe / next year)

   _____

6. (the patient / have the operation / today)

   _____

7. (it / take / few hours / to finish the project)

   _____

8. (he / be happy / about the promotion)

   _____

9. (she / be excited / about the new job)

   _____

10. (we / drive to work / together / every day)

    _____

11. (you / miss / me / next year)

_____

12. (I / get to work early / tomorrow morning)

_____

B Write *wh-* and *yes/no* questions for the answers.

1. _____ *What are you going to do Friday night?* _____

I'm going to <u>go to the movies</u> Friday night.

2. _____

Yes, we're going to do our homework together.

3. _____

They're going to go on vacation <u>in August</u>.

4. _____

No, they're not going to go to California.

5. _____

The meeting is going to take <u>two hours</u>.

6. _____

Yes, we're going to buy a new house.

7. _____

She's going to meet me <u>at 2:00</u>.

8. _____

No, he's not going to be late for class.

9. _____

I'm going to <u>get my hair cut</u> today.

10. _____

Yes, they're both going to be LPNs.

C Answer the questions with true information. (Answers will vary.)

1. What are you going to do tonight?

   _____

2. Where are you going to go tomorrow morning?

   _____

3. When are you going to have dinner?

   _____

4. Who are you going to talk to later?

   _____

5. How are you going to get to your next class?

   _____

PART TWO	The Future with the Present Progressive

A Write a sentence in the present progressive to describe plans. Use the words in parentheses and add a future time expression.

1. (walk the dog) _____ *I'm walking the dog at 6:00.* _____

2. (work late) _____

3. (study history) _____

4. (take kayaking classes) _____

5. (take a trip to Peru) _____

6. (observe an operation) _____

7. (get married) _____

8. (make a profit) _____

9. (the space shuttle takeoff) _____

10. (send a fax) _____

11. (surf the Web) _____

12. (take the dog to the vet) _____

13. (start a new exercise class) _____

B Complete the conversations with questions and answers about plans. Use *be going to* and the present progressive.

1. A: What are you doing tomorrow?

   B: _____ I'm going to a concert. _____ (go to a concert)

   A: _____

   B: I'm working.

2. A: Where are your parents going for vacation?

   B: _____ (to the Virgin Islands)

   A: _____

   B: I'm not going anywhere. I'm staying home.

3. A: _____

   B: I'm meeting with Andrea Garcia tomorrow.

   A: _____

   B: No, I'm not having lunch with her.

4. A: How long are you staying in Texas?

   B: _____ (one week)

   A: _____

   B: I'm traveling by plane.

5. A: _____

   B: She's having surgery next week.

   A: _____

   B: Yes, she's staying with me after the surgery.

Putting It Together

■ GRAMMAR

A Complete the conversations with questions and answers. Use *be going to* and the present progressive. (Answers may vary.)

Grandma: I can't believe this is your last year of nursing school!

Violet: I know! I ___ am going to be ___ (be) a nurse next year.

Grandma: When _____ (start) classes?

Violet: I _____ (go) back to Boston next week. My classes

_____ (start) the week after.

Grandma: Where _____ (stay) this year? In an apartment or in a dorm?

Violet: I'm _____ (be) in an apartment, but I'm going to eat on campus.

Grandma: That's a good idea. You _____ (have) a lot of privacy, but you _____ (have) to cook!

Violet: That's right! I _____ (be) very busy. I _____ (not have) time to cook good meals.

Grandma: Are you going to work?

Violet: Yes. Next week I _____ (work) in a hospital part time.

Grandma: I hope you _____ (have) time to do your homework.

Violet: Don't worry, Grandma. I'm going to work, go to classes, do my homework, and have a little fun on weekends, too.

B Rewrite the sentences with mistakes. If there are no mistakes, write "C."

1. I going to be a pilot next year!   _I'm going to be a pilot next year!_

2. She's no going to be ready at 2:00.   _____

3. We're being busy next week.   _____

4. Are you going to take a long time?   _____

5. She's going to doing her homework.   _____

6. You're working a lot next week.   _____

7. I not going to watch TV anymore.   _____

8. What you are going to do next year?   _____

9. They're taking a break from school.   _____

10. Who are you go to invite to the party?   _____

11. She's have friends over for dinner tonight.   _____

12. He says it's going to be fine!   _____

Find the words in the puzzle below and circle them.

```
T  V  D  M  R  O  F  I  N  U  A  Y  T  A  U
L  N  X  B  E  P  N  D  E  D  E  R  S  N  X
G  C  E  K  V  V  I  V  F  H  C  E  W  E  O
X  E  V  I  F  J  R  N  T  W  C  G  E  S  U
N  B  X  S  T  E  P  R  J  A  U  R  K  T  Q
N  U  H  D  S  A  U  H  O  R  N  U  Y  H  H
M  H  R  B  C  R  P  P  S  D  O  S  N  E  B
B  I  O  S  Y  N  E  D  O  C  T  O  R  T  M
S  A  X  W  E  R  F  B  S  B  F  M  G  I  I
B  G  F  Y  A  Y  Q  G  E  F  H  D  H  C  B
L  Q  A  T  J  M  H  F  O  P  X  S  G  Z  O
N  Q  I  X  Y  C  G  L  N  B  F  Z  P  D  O
M  O  W  F  Q  O  B  U  B  D  Y  N  V  C  K
N  G  O  K  E  A  D  H  D  P  L  U  S  X  O
M  Q  E  Z  R  V  W  J  I  Q  E  E  X  J  S
```

ANESTHETIC

DOCTOR

NURSE

OBSERVE

OPERATION

PATIENT

SURGERY

UNIFORM

WARD

PART ONE	The Future with *Will*

A Decide whether each statement is a prediction, a promise, a decision, or a plan.

1. I think I'll go to the store right now. *decision*

2. I'll work really hard in class this year. _____

3. The teacher will help you in a few minutes. _____

4. We won't need keyboards in the future. _____

5. Don't worry! We'll clean up the kitchen after we finish cooking. _____

6. Maria will go to Spain next year. _____

7. I will be your friend forever! _____

8. They'll never colonize Mars. _____

B Make predictions about the future. Write sentences with *will* using the words in parentheses. Add future time expressions.

1. (get married)

   I will get married when I am 35.

2. (read books)

   _____

3. (have cars that fly)

   _____

4. (listen to music)

   _____

5. (watch TV)

_____

6. (have children)

_____

C Make promises to yourself, friends, or your teacher. Use *will*.

1. _____ *I won't watch any TV during the week.* _____

2. _____

3. _____

4. _____

5. _____

6. _____

D Complete the sentences with predictions about your friends and family.

1. In six months _____ *my sister will have a boyfriend.* _____

2. Next week _____

3. Next month _____

4. In one year _____

5. In five years _____

6. In ten years _____

E Write *yes/no* and information questions for the answers.

1. _____ *Will you give me a ride to class tomorrow?* _____

   Yes, I'll give you a ride to class tomorrow.

2. _____

   Clara will not marry Juan Torres.

3. _____

   Yes, we'll come to dinner now.

4. _____

No, they won't study harder next year.

5. _____

We'll know the results of the test <u>next week</u>.

6. _____

Scientists will send someone <u>in 2012</u>.

7. _____

Yes, she'll answer your questions.

8. _____

It will take <u>many years</u> to put oxygen into the atmosphere.

PART TWO   **The Future with *There + Will Be***

A **Make predictions about our world. Use *there + will/will not* and the items in parentheses. Use the time phrase *in fifty* years.**

1. (computers) _____ *There will be computers in fifty years.* _____

2. (chalkboards) _____

3. (schools) _____

4. (telephones) _____

5. (gas-powered cars) _____

6. (single-family homes) _____

7. (marriage) _____

8. (fax machines) _____

9. (war) _____

10. (robots) _____

11. (only one language) _____

12. (space tourism) _____

13. (solar-powered cars) _____

B **Make predictions about daily events. Use *there* + *will/will not* and the words in parentheses.**

1. (no meeting next week) _____ *There won't be a meeting next week.* _____

2. (dance next Saturday) _____

3. (no homework tonight) _____

4. (no time to take a break) _____

5. (money for a new computer) _____

6. (no money for a new school) _____

7. (a parade on the weekend) _____

8. (an ESL conference in Florida) _____

9. (no classes tonight) _____

10. (a taxi waiting at the airport) _____

11. (changes in the schedule) _____

12. (dinner after the meeting) _____

13. (no free parking) _____

Putting It Together

GRAMMAR

Unscramble the sentences to complete the conversation.

Ben: the basketball game / tonight / you / going to / are

_____ *Are you going to the basketball game tonight?* _____

Simon: I don't know. Will there be a lot of people at the game from our class?

Ben: will / yes / there / be _____

Simon: going / your / with us / sister / is _____

Ben: I don't know.

Simon: to / ask / you / go / will / her _____

Ben: Yes, I will.

Simon: food / there / at / the game / be / will _____

Ben: I think there will be some food.

Simon: there / what / food / of / kind / will / be _____

Ben: There will probably be hot dogs, hamburgers, and soft drinks.

Simon: me / money / will / lend / you _____

I don't have money for food.

Ben: won't / any / money / you / lend / I _____

Simon: back / you / I / pay / will _____

I promise.

Ben: you / no / won't _____

You still owe me 20 dollars.

Simon: Oh, that's right. I'm sorry. I'll pay you back.

Ben: So, are you going to go tonight?

Simon: guess / I / yes / will / I _____

■ VOCABULARY

Find the words in the puzzle below and circle them.

E	P	S	J	A	T	Z	C	X	S
R	L	H	U	T	B	O	M	E	F
E	A	K	B	R	R	B	C	C	Z
H	N	V	M	E	F	R	G	I	D
P	T	X	P	V	U	A	Y	H	P
S	B	C	N	O	X	G	C	G	C
O	E	M	S	S	J	P	Y	E	Q
M	G	E	B	R	E	A	T	H	E
T	R	J	U	W	M	F	R	D	C
A	G	B	Q	X	C	A	Q	N	A

ATMOSPHERE

BREATHE

CORE

DIG

PLANT

RESOURCES

SURFACE

Possibility: *May, Might, Could;* Future Conditional with *Will, May, Might*

PART ONE	Possibility: *May, Might, Could*

A Read the paragraph and then read each statement below. Based on the paragraph, decide whether the statements are true (T), false (F), or possible (P).

Sarah's Dilemma

It couldn't be Wednesday already! I might not have time to do anything this week. I may have to stay in every night and finish the report for the sales conference. I might not have time to finish it. It could be too late already. My boss might get angry.

1. It's Wednesday. _____T_____

2. Sarah is going to be able to go to the movies this week. _____

3. Sarah is going to stay home every night this week. _____

4. She probably won't finish the report. _____

5. It's not too late. _____

6. Her boss isn't going to be angry. _____

B What might these people be someday? Write a sentence with *may, might,* or *could.*

1. Karen goes to the movies twice a week. (actor)

   _____She might be an actor someday._____

2. Henry is a senator. (president)

   _____

3. Cesar practices the guitar every day. (famous)

   _____

4. Olivia enjoys talking with people. (talk show host)

_____

5. Sara and Yasmin like playing soccer. (professional soccer players)

_____

6. Roberto likes working with young children. (teacher)

_____

C **Choose the best answer.**

1. Mrs. Jones doesn't use the telephone.
   a. She might be the caller. (b) She couldn't be   c. She called.
                                    the caller.

2. Are you going to the movies with me tonight?
   a. I go to the movies   b. I went to the   c. I may go with you.
      every night.   movies.

3. Maria doesn't have a car.
   a. She could drive to work. b. She might drive   c. She couldn't drive
                                   to work.   to work.

4. What might I find at a children's museum?
   a. You might not.   b. You could not   c. You might find
                                 find anything.   dinosaurs.

5. Where could I get my car repaired?
   a. At Joe's Garage.   b. You might not.   c. You'll get it repaired.

6. I saw Graciela five minutes ago; she looked great.
   a. She may be sick.   b. She couldn't be sick. c. She is sick.

A   Match the *if* clause with its secondary clause.

1. If you practice every day, _e_   a. we may have to leave without them.

2. If we only speak English in class, ___   b. he won't have money to buy a house.

3. If they don't arrive soon, ___   c. she won't get a good job.

4. If he buys a new car, ___   d. you might get there late.

5. If I learn English, ___   e. you'll improve a lot.

6. If she doesn't finish school, ___   f. she won't be able to leave the country.

7. If you walk to work, ___   g. the instructor might ask us to leave.

8. If we talk in class, ___   h. we'll learn it a lot faster.

9. If she doesn't get a passport, ___   i. you might get a ticket.

10. If you drive too fast, ___   j. I might get a better job.

B   Use the two groups of words to make a future conditional sentence. Use *will, may, might,* or *could* in your sentences.

1. look younger / you get a haircut

You'll look younger if you get a haircut.

2. save money / we don't eat out

_____

3. you exercise more / lose weight

_____

4. I get two jobs / make more money

_____

5. you start a new hobby / make new friends

_____

6. meet more people / we go out more

_____

7. feel better / you quit smoking

   _____

8. she goes to sleep earlier / have more energy

   _____

Putting It Together

■ GRAMMAR

A Rewrite the sentences with mistakes. If there are no mistakes, write "C."

1. Where we could go for vacation this year?   _Where could we go for vacation this year?_

2. Could Elena be the winner of the lottery?   _____

3. If you are healthy, you'll be happy.   _____

4. I mightn't go to class tonight.   _____

5. Might you go to dinner with me?   _____

6. If they will find evidence, it might help the case.   _____

7. May you give me a ride to work?   _____

8. If you might practice a lot, you will learn English quickly.   _____

9. My boss could give me a raise this year.   _____

10. If they begin the investigation today, it could take a long time to get the results?   _____

B The words and phrases that are underlined may have mistakes. If there is a mistake, make a correction.

Hi Katie!

Sorry I didn't <u>wrote</u> ^*write* earlier. Some friends <u>might visit</u> this weekend so <u>I</u> really busy planning. If they <u>will come</u>, we <u>may spend</u> one day in the city. We <u>maybe go</u> to a museum here in town. <u>If we go</u> to the Town Museum, <u>we'll see</u> a great exhibit on forensic science. I <u>read</u> about the exhibit on the museum's Web site. We <u>could also go</u> to the beach. But they're from Miami, so they <u>might not want to go</u> to the beach. Anyway, if they <u>didn't come</u>, my husband and I will finish painting the living room.

I'll write more on Monday!

Love,
Amanda

■ VOCABULARY

Complete the clues and solve the puzzle.

Across

4. The detective gathered the _____ .
5. He saw the robber.

Down

1. The police arrested the _____ .
2. She's in charge of the investigation.
3. The murderer used _____ to kill her husband.

The Zero Article with Geographical Features; The Definite Article with Geographical Features

PART ONE	The Zero Article with Geographical Features

A Complete the conversations with *a*, *the*, or *Ø* (no article).

1. A: I went to ___*a*___ famous lake this weekend.

   B: Where is _____ lake?

   A: It's in New York.

   B: Did you go to _____ Lake Champlain?

   A: Yes! It's _____ beautiful lake!

2. A: I went to Rapa Nui for vacation last year.

   B: What's Rapa Nui?

   A: It's _____ island.

   B: Oh! Are you talking about _____ Easter Island?

   A: Yes, that's the name of _____ island in English.

3. A: Have you been to _____ Rhode Island?

   B: What is it? Is it _____ famous island?

   A: Not really. It's _____ smallest state in the United States. It's near _____ Connecticut.

   B: No. And I haven't been to _____ Connecticut, either.

4. A: _____ Tampa Bay is very beautiful.

   B: _____ Tampa Bay is in _____ Florida, right?

   A: Yes, it is. I like _____ Tampa more than _____ Miami. What about you?

   B: I don't know _____ Florida very well.

5. A: Did you know that Laura is from _____ Peru?

   B: Yes, I did. She's from _____ big city, I think.

   A: She's from _____ Lima, _____ capital.

   B: I would like to visit her country someday.

B **Write the name of a geographical feature. Then write a sentence about the feature.**

1. Name of a mountain near you: _____ Bear Mountain _____
   _____ Bear Mountain is the highest mountain in Connecticut. _____

2. Name of a lake near you: _____
   _____

3. Name of an island near you: _____
   _____

4. Name of a country you have visited: _____
   _____

5. Name of a city you have visited: _____
   _____

6. Name of a state you have visited: _____
   _____

PART TWO	The Definite Article with Geographical Features

A **Complete the sentences with _the_ or Ø.**

1. I lived across from __the__ Farmington River for 23 years.

2. _____ Lake Wobegon is not a real lake.

3. There are many rivers that run into _____ Amazon.

4. Kansas is one of the states in the region called _____ Great Plains.

5. We're going to _____ Hawaiian Islands for our anniversary.

6. _____ Mt. Hood is a volcano in Oregon.

7. _____ Cascades are a mountain range in Oregon.

8. I saw _____ Mt. Fuji from the train.

9. _____ Atlantic is smaller than _____ Pacific.

10. We're going to be staying in a cabin in _____ Rocky Mountains.

11. _____ Salt Lake City is surrounded by mountains.

B Complete the sentences using the words in parentheses and *the* or *a/an*.

1. (ocean) I would like to take a cruise on _____ *the ocean.* _____

2. (river) I would like to canoe down _____

3. (group of islands) I would like to sail to _____

4. (mountain range) I would like to see _____

5. (region) I would like to visit _____

6. (harbor) I would like to visit _____

7. (canyon) I would like to visit _____

8. (gulf) I would like to visit _____

 ## Putting It Together

■ **G R A M M A R**

A Find the mistakes. Write in the correct answers.

Dear Adriana,

Our tour of ^ *the* United States is amazing. This week we're in the Arizona. I'm writing to you from Grand Canyon. It's so beautiful. I can see Colorado River. River runs through seven states: Colorado, New Mexico, the Utah, Wyoming, Arizona, California, and the Nevada. Most of the water in river comes from melted snow in Rocky Mountains. The river also flows through Mojave Desert and Sonoran Desert. River flows from mountains in west to Gulf of California in the Mexico. (Gulf is also called the Sea of Cortez.)

Next week, I'll write you from the Florida. We're going to spend several days in Everglades!

Love,
Amalia

Use the clues to solve the puzzle.

Across

2. the Andes

4. Sydney

5. Hawiian

Down

1. the Grand

3. the Panama

The Present Perfect with *Be*;
The Present Perfect with Other Verbs

PART ONE	The Present Perfect with *Be*

A **Complete the statements with the present perfect of *be*.**

1. I _____*have been*_____ a teacher for 15 years.

2. You _____ a great friend.

3. Pablo _____ a carpenter since 1994.

4. My mother _____ married two times.

5. We _____ involved in the theater for many years.

6. My friends _____ at my house all week.

7. They _____ in rehearsal since 3:00.

8. Anne _____ in many plays.

9. He _____ early every day this week.

10. I _____ really happy this year.

B **Complete the statements in the affirmative or negative to make them true for you. Use contractions.**

1. I _____*haven't been*_____ to the Vatican.

2. I _____ to Alaska.

3. I _____ to New York City.

4. I _____ married.

5. I _____ divorced.

6. I _____ in love many times.

7. I _____ to a play.

8. I _____ to the movies this week.

9. I _____ on a roller coaster.

10. I _____ late to class this semester.

C Complete the sentences with *for* or *since.*

1. We've been married _____for_____ 5 years.

2. My family has been in Connecticut _____ 1961.

3. I've been a member of the gym _____ two years.

4. They haven't been in our town _____ a long time.

5. Betty has been at home _____ a few hours.

6. Juan has been in preschool _____ September.

7. Juliana has been in our family _____ July 25, 2005.

PART TWO	The Present Perfect with Other Verbs

A Complete the sentences with the present perfect of the verb in parentheses. If necessary, use either *for* or *since* in the second blank.

1. We _____have wanted_____ (want) to visit the Grand Canyon for a long time.

2. Michael _____ (work) at home _____ last year.

3. Abdul _____ (not retire) yet.

4. My sisters _____ (sing) in a rock band _____ many years.

5. She _____ (not live) in our town _____ a long time.

6. I _____ (not know) you very long.

7. My professor _____ (write) two books.

8. We _____ (learn) a lot living in Mexico.

9. I _____ (think) a lot about you _____ high school.

10. They _____ (see) that movie _____ a few times.

11. Fred _____ (teach) English in Asia _____ last year.

12. The instructors _____ (offer) to help us after class.

13. I _____ (quit) my job three times this year.

14. My best friend _____ (have) heart surgery.

B **Write true sentences about yourself with the words below. If possible, use time expressions.**

1. work / two years

   _____ *I've worked at the bookstore for two years.* _____

2. save money / this year

   _____

3. exercise / today

   _____

4. speak to my family / today

   _____

5. make new friends / this year

   _____

6. study English / every day

   _____

7. sing in the shower / this week

   _____

8. sleep well / this week

   _____

9. look at my e-mail / today

   _____

10. go to the theater / this year

    _____

Putting It Together

■ GRAMMAR

A Complete the paragraph with the appropriate form of the verb in parentheses.

Bernadette Peters _____*is*_____ (be) one of the most famous stage actors on Broadway. She _____ (star) in many musicals. She _____ (win) many awards. She _____ (debut) in her first musical in 1967 and she still _____ (perform) leading roles on Broadway today. She _____ (be) not only an actress, but she also _____ (sing). She _____ (record) six albums. She _____ (act) in many movies and _____ (appear) in many TV shows.

B Rewrite the sentences with mistakes. If there are no mistakes, write "C."

1. I not been to class in a long time. *I haven't been to class in a long time.*

2. We have learn a lot in class this year. _____

3. They haven't live here since a long time. _____

4. My favorite song hasn't played on the radio at all today. _____

5. Paul and Audrey haven't spoken in three days. _____

6. I've work every night this week. _____

7. My sister has seen this movie four times. _____

8. I haven't wrote any e-mail today. _____

9. My parents haven't never been to the United States. _____

10. Anika has performed in several school plays. _____

11. Mr. Garcia's been a police officer for ten years. _____

12. They've been divorced since five years. _____

Find the words in the puzzle below and circle them.

```
R  F  Y  M  A  R  A  G  B  N  Z  F  E  Q  K
E  L  Q  H  H  B  H  T  A  V  U  G  D  J  C
H  Z  A  P  A  K  Q  I  J  B  A  M  O  D  G
E  U  F  C  W  E  C  V  X  T  S  H  R  B  T
A  N  W  L  I  I  R  B  S  X  T  R  E  J  E
R  C  O  T  N  S  S  P  O  T  L  I  G  H  T
S  X  A  H  N  C  U  P  T  L  L  O  A  N  S
A  B  C  R  S  M  E  M  W  X  O  E  N  K  M
L  E  I  L  P  R  J  W  V  I  Q  I  A  Y  W
T  S  R  O  A  E  J  M  K  Z  Q  D  M  F  J
J  N  H  T  N  N  N  R  E  T  A  E  H  T  W
I  I  O  O  N  U  F  T  D  X  D  N  C  L  S
S  R  I  T  W  I  P  P  E  L  X  D  H  N  H
L  M  X  S  O  U  N  D  M  R  X  G  I  H  R
N  F  B  J  R  F  Q  A  A  U  Q  V  V  A  U
```

CARPENTER

MANAGER

MUSICAL

OPERATOR

REHEARSAL

SHOW

SOUND

SPOTLIGHT

STAGE

TECHNICIAN

THEATER

The Present Perfect: Questions;
The Present Perfect: *Ever, Never*

PART ONE	The Present Perfect: Questions

A Write *yes/no* questions in the present perfect tense. Then complete the short answers.

1. you / see / the movie *Titanic*

   _____ Have you seen the movie Titanic? _____

   Yes, _____ I have. _____

2. your mother / visit / you / in the United States

   _____

   No, she _____

3. your instructor / give / you / a quiz / yet

   _____

   Yes, he _____

4. we / complete / the homework

   _____

   No, we _____

5. you / audition / for a movie

   _____

   Yes, I _____

6. they / stay / at your house / before

   _____

   No, they _____

7. Molly / be / to the new theater

   _____

   Yes, she _____

B **Write the interview questions for actor/director Tom Gem.**

Interviewer: _____How long have you been an actor?_____

Tom Gem: I've been an actor for 13 years.

Interviewer: _____

Tom Gem: I've been married for four years.

Interviewer: _____

Tom Gem: I've always wanted to be a director.

Interviewer: _____

Tom Gem: I've waited my whole life to direct a movie.

Interviewer: _____

Tom Gem: I've known the actor Johnny Jo Theakston for ten years.

Interviewer: _____

Tom Gem: I've wanted to work with Johnny Jo Theakston ever since we met.

PART TWO	The Present Perfect: *Ever, Never*

A **Complete the conversations. Use *ever*.**

1.   Gina: ____Have____ you _ever gotten_ (get) an athlete's autograph?

    Simon: Yes, _____

2.   Abel: _____ your mother _____ (go) to a rock concert?

    Shania: No, _____

3. Jennifer: _____ your friends _____ (hear) you sing?

    Drew: Yes, _____

4.   Carlos: _____ we _____ (do) the present perfect?

    Juan: No, _____

5. Antonio: _____ your brother _____ (pick) you up from work?

    Paola: Yes, _____

6.   Aiden: _____ you _____ (travel) to Europe?

    Clare: No, _____

7. Tomas: _____ Ms. Ramirez_____ (miss) a class?

   Pat: Yes, _____

8. Anne: _____ you _____ (have) a pet?

   Sandra: No, _____

B Write five things you <u>have never done</u>. Use the present perfect and *never*.

1. _____ *I have never climbed Mt. Everest.* _____

2. _____

3. _____

4. _____

5. _____

C Write five things you <u>have done</u>. Use the present perfect.

1. _____ *I have been on an airplane.* _____

2. _____

3. _____

4. _____

5. _____

D Write five questions for your teacher. Use the present perfect with *ever*.

1. _____ *Have you ever been to a different country?* _____

2. _____

3. _____

4. _____

5. _____

Putting It Together

■ **GRAMMAR**

A Rewrite the sentences with mistakes. If there are no mistakes, write "C."

1. I haven't never ridden a bicycle.   *I have never ridden a bicycle.*

2. Have you worked in a restaurant?   _____

3. Have they ever say "thank you"? _____

4. I haven't ever been on a plane. _____

5. How long you wanted to be a teacher? _____

6. Have you ever meet a famous actor? _____

7. I haven't exercise in a long time. _____

8. We haven't ever spoken by phone. _____

9. Have your friends study for the test? _____

10. Never she has met a famous person. _____

11. How long has Eva been your friend? _____

12. Has he ever call you? _____

■ VOCABULARY

Unscramble each of the clue words. Take the letters that appear in circles and unscramble them to see the final question below.

SUIDTO   ☐ ◯ ☐ ◯

RAMCEA   ☐ ◯ ☐ ◯ ◯

TECRIDRO   ☐ ☐ ☐ ◯ ☐ ◯ ◯

SATR   ☐ ◯ ◯ ☐

ANF   ☐ ◯ ◯

TIRSCP   ☐ ◯ ◯ ☐ ◯

NUIDOTIA   ◯ ☐ ◯ ☐ ☐ ◯ ◯

H ☐ V ☐ Y ☐ ☐ V E ☐ W ☐ ☐ E ☐ ☐ ☐ B E ☐ ☐

☐ ☐ ☐ ☐ ☐ ?

Superlative Adjectives;
Superlative Adverbs

PART ONE	Superlative Adjectives

A Write the superlative form of the adjective.

1. cloudy _the cloudiest_

2. healthy _____

3. good _____

4. long _____

5. big _____

6. serious _____

7. tall _____

8. interesting _____

9. humid _____

10. difficult _____

11. far _____

12. polluted _____

13. hot _____

14. attractive _____

15. dirty _____

16. bad _____

17. nice _____

18. windy _____

B Describe people, things, or places in your country using the superlatives above. Use prepositional phrases. Use *"one of the"* in seven of the sentences.

1. _____ Lima is the cloudiest city in Peru. _____

2. _____

3. _____

4. _____

5. _____

6. _____

7. _____

8. _____

9. _____

10. _____

11. _____

12. _____

13. _____

14. _____

A Complete the sentences with the superlative form of the adverb.

1. The diet works (efficiently) _**most efficiently**_ when you don't eat after 8:00 PM.

2. She runs (well) _____ in the morning.

3. My brother studied (hard) _____ for the exam.

4. They were talking (loudly) _____ of all the guests during dinner.

5. The teacher always arrives (early) _____ .

6. The contestant from Venezuela answered the question (quickly) _____ .

7. She cried (hard) _____ after her father died.

8. The newlyweds danced (elegantly) _____ of all the couples at the reception.

9. Mario walked ten miles today. He walked (far) _____ .

10. We drive (recklessly) _____ when we're tired.

B Write true answers to the questions.

1. When do you sleep the best?

   _____ _I sleep the best in the morning._ _____

2. Who exercises the most?

   _____

3. Who runs the fastest in your family?

   _____

4. What restaurant do you eat at most often?

   _____

5. Who speaks English the best in your class?

   _____

6. Who speaks the most softly in your house?

   _____

7. What class do you attend the most regularly?

   _____

8. Who in the class does their homework the most cheerfully?

   _____

9. When do you eat the best?

   _____

Putting It Together

GRAMMAR

A Write true sentences about your country using the phrases in parentheses.

1. (highest mountain)
   Aconcagua is the highest mountain in Argentina.

2. (warmest city)

   _____

3. (tallest building)

   _____

4. (best soccer team)

   _____

5. (place that attracts the most tourists)

   _____

6. (best author)

   _____

7. (most prestigious university)

_____

8. (the newspaper with the highest circulation)

_____

B **Rewrite the sentences with mistakes. If there are no mistakes, write "C."**

1. I run more fastest in cold weather.   _I run faster in cold weather._

2. Carbon dioxide is the bad greenhouse gas.   _____

3. Albert Einstein is the more famous scientist in history.   _____

4. She treats the children very gently.   _____

5. Sara speaks the most quietest in the class.   _____

6. Today I arrived the earliest.   _____

7. What is the big problem in the world today?   _____

8. Rochester, New York, is the snowy city in the United States.   _____

Unscramble each of the clue words. Use the numbered letters to complete the sentence at the bottom.

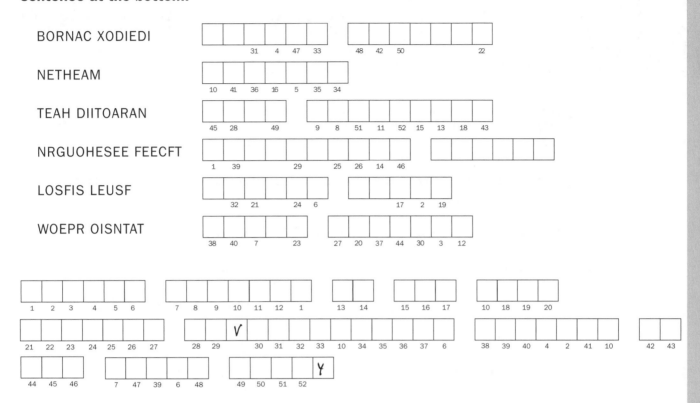

BORNAC XODIEDI

31 4 47 33   48 42 50   22

NETHEAM

10 41 36 16 5 35 34

TEAH DIITOARAN

45 28   49   9 8 51 11 52 15 13 18 43

NRGUOHESEE FEECFT

1 39   29   25 26 14 46

LOSFIS LEUSF

32 21   24 6   17 2 19

WOEPR OISNTAT

38 40 7   23   27 20 37 44 30 3 12

1 2 3 4 5 6   7 8 9 10 11 12 1   13 14   15 16 17   10 18 19 20

21 22 23 24 25 26 27   28 29   30 31 32 33 10 34 35 36 37 6   38 39 40 4 2 41 10   42 43

44 45 46   7 47 39 6 48   49 50 51 52

Review: From Past To Present;
Review: From Present to Future

PART ONE   Review: From Past to Present

A Complete the sentences with the correct tense. In some cases, more than one answer may be correct.

1. We (talk) _____ talked _____ on the phone yesterday for more than an hour.

2. James (not live) _____ in France for a long time.

3. I always (take) _____ a shower in the morning.

4. Gwyn (visit) _____ her parents when she was in Wales.

5. Her parents really (want) _____ to learn English.

6. I (study) _____ music for two years.

7. They (do) _____ their laundry right now.

8. You (not be) _____ late; you (be) _____ early.

9. Carina and Jose (work) _____ at the library.

10. I (wait) _____ an hour for you.

11. They (not do) _____ their homework last night.

12. She (teach) _____ English since 1994.

13. We (not have) _____ class today.

14. My father (build) _____ a house now in Florida.

15. When we (be) _____ young, my family (live) _____ in Ireland.

16. I (like) _____ rock music.

17. My brother (drive) _____ when the tree fell across the road.

18. My friends sometimes (eat) _____ lunch in the park.

19. Some students (talk) _____ in class right now.

20. I (know) _____ my best friend for over twenty years.

B **Write the questions for the answers.**

1. _____ *Did you walk to school today?* _____

   Yes, I walked to school today.

2. _____

   My parents came to the United States <u>when I was three years old</u>.

3. _____

   My sister didn't call me today.

4. _____

   <u>A friend</u> helped me prepare for the test.

5. _____

   Absolutely. We're very happy.

6. _____

   Angela is <u>home</u> now.

7. _____

   <u>He</u> is my brother.

8. _____

   No, they aren't students.

9. _____

   Sometimes we get to work <u>by bus</u>.

10. _____

    Yes, I always wake up early.

11. _____

    I wake up <u>at 6:00 AM</u>.

12. _____

    No, you don't have to work today.

13. _____

Margot washes the dishes every night.

14. _____

They're watching a movie.

15. _____

No, Alan isn't talking on his cell phone.

16. _____

Carolina is doing homework.

17. _____

When we got home, the dogs were sleeping.

18. _____

I was driving home when I heard the news.

19. _____

In 1980, my family was living in Uruguay.

20. _____

No, I haven't heard of Trader Smith's supermarket.

21. _____

No, my grandmother has never been on a plane.

22. _____

We've lived in Chicago for two months.

23. _____

I've gone to the museum, but I haven't gone to the park yet.

PART TWO   **Review: From Present to Future**

A **Complete the sentences with the present progressive, *be going to*, or *will*. In some cases, more than one answer may be correct.**

1. We (travel) _____*are traveling*_____ to Colombia next month.

2. My company (hire) _____ 500 more employees.

3. In the future, people (not read) _____ newspapers.

4. In the next year or two, natural gas prices (fall) _____ .

5. The population of Spanish speakers in the United States (continue) _____ to increase.

6. I (help) _____ you pass your exam.

7. Tomorrow we (go) _____ to the new mall after class.

8. Next year the school (give) _____ more financial aid.

9. I think housing prices (rise) _____ in the spring.

10. There's a shortage of teachers. I think teachers' salaries (increase) _____ .

11. I (love) _____ you forever.

12. Someday we (not need) _____ telephones.

B Unscramble the words to make a question. Then complete the answers.

1. marry / me / you / will

   _____ Will you marry me? _____

   Yes, _____

2. taking / a vacation / you / this year / are

   _____

   No, _____

3. she / new /going / computer / buy / is / to / a

   _____

   Yes, _____

4. for / future / people / in / the / are / will / travel / to / the moon / vacation

   _____

   No, _____

5. always/ you / my / will / be / best friend

   _____

   Yes, _____

C Write true sentences in the future tense.

1. a promise with *will*

   _____ I will never miss class again. _____

2. a future plan with *be going to*

   _____

3. a prediction about the near future

   _____

4. a negative prediction about the future

   _____

Putting It Together

■ GRAMMAR

A Complete the questions.

1. A: _____Are you going_____ to go to Sandra's house after class?
   B: I don't know.

2. A: _____ stay with me when I'm in the hospital?
   B: Yes, I will.

3. A: _____ see the debate on TV last night?
   B: Yes, I did.

4. A: _____ thinking about me?
   B: Yes, I am.

5. A: _____ pick me up after class?
   B: Sam's going to pick you up.

6. A: _____ seen the new Julia Roberts movie?
   B: No, I haven't.

7. A: _____ doing when you heard about the plane crash?
   B: I was taking a shower.

8. A: _____ doing tomorrow?
   B: I'm buying a new car.

9. A: _____ people going to stop buying CDs eventually?

   B: Yes, they are. They're going to buy more music digitally, online.

10. A: _____ be cars in the future?

    B: Yes, there will.

B Complete the conversation with the correct form of the verb in parentheses.

Zury: Hi, Jen. I'm glad you're here. I _____*called*_____ (call) you this morning.

Jen: Why did you call?

Zury: I _____ (want) you to go somewhere with me.

Jen: Where are you going?

Zury: I _____ (go) to the mall to buy a CD.

Jen: I _____ (buy) any CDs in a long time.

Zury: Neither have I.

Jen: Now, I usually _____ (buy) music online.

Zury: Me, too.

Jen: I think fewer and fewer people _____ (buy) CDs.

Zury: I agree. In the future, there _____ (not be) CDs—only digital files online.

Jen: Yes, the record companies _____ (manufacture) fewer CDs.

Zury: Anyway . . . let's go to the mall. The music store is having a big sale today.

Jen: OK. I _____ (go)!

Find the words in the puzzle below and circle them.

```
M   D   R   E   T   H   K   Z   A   J   F   S   T   A   V
H   J   N   G   I   L   E   T   G   R   T   C   X   L   N
X   F   M   A   P   O   V   Y   A   P   K   Z   V   J   H
A   U   H   U   L   K   M   N   E   Y   C   J   W   H   C
Q   Q   P   G   T   T   C   F   D   O   B   U   Y   Y   M
D   G   Y   N   E   E   O   N   G   E   R   M   A   N   Y
E   E   D   A   E   T   A   C   I   N   U   M   M   O   C
N   K   N   L   C   L   C   L   S   N   M   R   W   F   U
G   Y   O   M   E   V   F   Z   T   Q   Y   V   O   H   P
L   B   Q   R   A   E   C   L   W   K   R   Y   T   S   C
A   X   I   Q   D   R   D   L   K   Z   K   G   I   K   L
N   K   J   W   T   U   K   I   V   P   J   R   B   N   X
D   H   V   O   Z   T   N   J   E   R   M   T   O   G   A
N   F   H   V   M   N   H   N   P   Z   V   K   P   Y   E
S   E   L   A   W   T   T   G   G   W   V   C   R   U   K
```

COMMUNICATE

DENMARK

ENGLAND

FRANCE

GERMANY

IRELAND

LANGUAGE

SCOTLAND

WALES

I. Expressing an Opinion

A Read about how to express an opinion.

Giving an opinion	Examples	Supporting statement
I think ...	**I think** tourism is good for the country.	Tourism brings in lots of money, which is good for the economy.
I believe ...	**I believe** nurses should get more money.	Nurses work long hours and save people's lives.
In my opinion, ...	**In my opinion,** we will never go to Mars.	Space travel is too expensive.
Note: The phrase *In my opinion* always has a comma after it.		

B Match the opinion with the supporting statement.

___ 1. I think that the Internet is good.   a. It does not work for people in poverty.

___ 2. I believe he may be the murderer.   b. It helps people communicate more easily.

___ 3. In my opinion, capitalism is bad.   c. His fingerprints are at the crime scene.

II. Giving Reasons and Examples

C Read about giving reasons and examples.

To give reasons in a paragraph, use **For example** and **For instance.** Use reasons to give additional information about a supporting sentence. **For example** and **For instance** are always followed by commas.

> Many tourists visit Florida. They come to see the interesting cities, amusement parks, and beach resorts in the state. For example, Orlando attracts 44 million visitors every year.

Topic sentence: *Many tourists visit Florida.*
Supporting sentence: *They come to see the interesting cities, amusement parks, and beach resorts in the state.*
Reason or example: *For example, Orlando attracts 44 million visitors every year.*

D Complete the sentences by giving examples.

1. There are many reasons global warming is bad.

   _____

2. The English language has changed a lot over the years.

   _____

3. Tom Cruise has been in many movies.

   _____

4. My sister has had many jobs in a theater.

   _____

III. Writing a Paragraph

E Read the paragraph below. There are 5 errors in forming opinions and reasons. Correct the errors.

> In my opine global warming is not a big problem. I think that a warmer climate could be good. Example, in northern Europe a warmer climate will mean farmers can grow more crops. I believe, that scientists will find a way to help people close to the shore. For instance—people could live on floating cities. In conclusion, I think people will find ways to cope with global warming.

F Write a paragraph giving your opinions about global warming.

G Check your paragraph. Use the checklist.

	Yes	No
Good paragraph form (see p. 51)		
Good punctuation (see p. 51)		
Topic, supporting, concluding sentences (see p. 102)		
Giving an opinion language		
Reason language		
Grammar from lessons 21–30		

H **Rewrite your paragraph.**